THE YONI

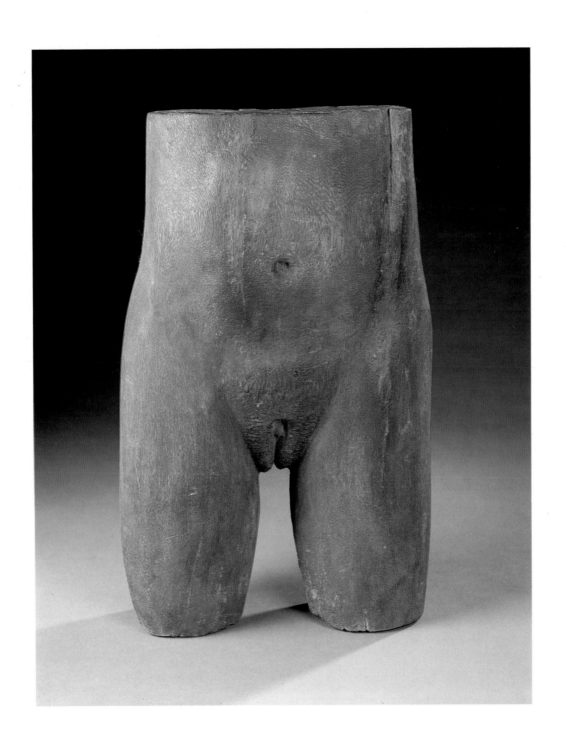

THE YONI

SACRED SYMBOL OF
FEMALE CREATIVE POWER

RUFUS C. CAMPHAUSEN

INNER TRADITIONS
ROCHESTER, VERMONT

INNER TRADITIONS INTERNATIONAL

ONE PARK STREET
ROCHESTER, VERMONT 05767

---

*Some of the practices and techniques described in this book or recommended by pre-AIDS
authorities quoted herein should be considered unsafe sexual practices if either partner is infected with
any transmittable disease. Furthermore, some of the practices and techniques described in this book are,
although common practices around the world, prohibited in some states and by certain institutions of the
United States and perhaps elsewhere. Before you attempt to engage in any of these practices,
please consult at least two physicians and two lawyers—just to be on the safe side.*

LIBRARY OF CONGRESS CATALOGING-IN-PUBLICATION DATA
Camphausen, Rufus C.
The yoni : sacred symbol of female creative power / Rufus C. Camphausen
p.   cm.
Includes bibliographical references and index.
ISBN 0-89281-562-0
1. Vulva—Religious aspects. 2. Women and religion. 3. Goddess religion. I. Title.
BL458.C34   1996   96-342
291.2'12—dc20   CIP
Printed and bound by Replika Press Pvt. Ltd, India

10 9 8 7 6 5 4 3 2

Text design and layout by Bonnie F. Atwater
This book was typeset in Berling Agency with Koch Antiqua and Copperplate as display typefaces.

DEDICATION

▼

This book is dedicated to Mahadevi, the Great Goddess,
and to all the other Goddesses who dance
in heaven and on earth as her manifestations.

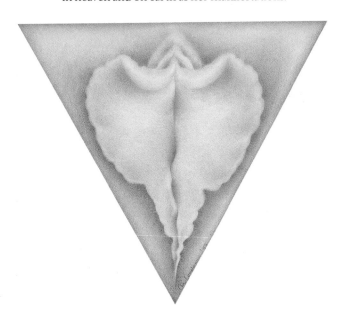

Contents

▼

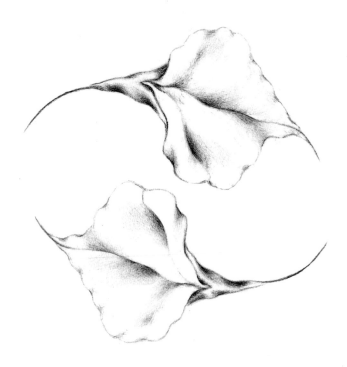

Anna, Apolonia, Aśka, Biggie, Christiane, Christina, Diana,

Doris, Elke, Eva, Gabi, Gertrud, Gisela, Giselle, Habibi,

Heidi, Helga, Inge, Irmgard, Jennifer, Judith, Kirsti,

Linda, Lorraine, Maaike, Maria, Marianne,

Marlo, Odile, Ophira, Raja, Rana, Ranva,

Reinhilde, Sabine, Sachiko, Safala,

Saga, Sissie, Sue, Supapon,

Sybille, Sylvia, Sylvie,

Tara, Uschi, and

Visarjana

▼

ACKNOWLEDGMENTS

▼

The most excellent place for practicing men
is wherever there is a gathering of practicing women;
There, all the magical powers will be attained.

CAKRASAMVARA TANTRA

For more than twenty-five years I have devoted much time and energy to the study of other cultures, especially their religions—often Goddess-oriented—and their sociosexual mores. This research was fueled to a great extent not only by a personal need to liberate myself from the conditionings most of us receive during childhood and through early education, but also by a deep desire to understand women as best I could—body, mind, and soul. Although I have always known this goal to be essentially impossible for any man (and perhaps even for most women) to realize, I believe that one should at least try to get as close to such an understanding as possible.

It is in part due to these interests that I have come to write this book, long overdue in Western culture. I had not really given consideration to the possibility that I would be its author until Ehud Sperling, the publisher at Inner Traditions International, invited me to create this work. For that reason and for other more practical ones, this book would not have been born without the help and stimulation I have received from the team of women and men at Inner Traditions. I would here like to applaud the vision and efforts of this team, which have made the first twenty years of Inner Traditions International's existence so successful.

Mostly, though, this book and the views expressed in it would never have seen the light of day were it not for my lifelong association with many women of all colors and ages, mostly as lovers and intimate friends, sometimes as trusted colleagues and associates. I want to thank all those women who have inspired me (see previous page). More than through my intellectual studies and efforts, it is through these women that I have come to appreciate the natural wisdom of the ancients.

The most special acknowledgments, blessings, and appreciation are reserved for Christina—my lover, friend, companion, and wife. I thank her not only for sustaining me with her love, understanding, and practical help throughout my work on this book, but, even more important, for truly and intimately sharing my enthusiasm for this topic and providing me with the emotional freedom to pursue it fully.

In preparing this book I have drawn on the inspiration and specialized material provided by others, both friends and strangers, who came to know about this work during the course of its creation. I thank Vincent Dame for giving me access to his extensive artwork collection and library, and for making the exceptional artwork he does. I thank Denish for his invaluable information, for his critical and supportive suggestions, and for his art and poems. Thank you to Annemarie Bokma, Ingrid van Hoof, Ton Kocken, and Ineke Schouwstra for providing photographic material; to Marianne for her translations from French; to Annelies and Beer for reports from Assam; and to Ellie for providing me with the beautiful images from Koh Samui.

Last but not least, I would like to express my appreciation and gratitude to Jeanie Levitan, Lee Wood, and Susan Davidson, editors at Inner Traditions, who by their professional experience and personal qualities have helped shape this work.

▼

INTRODUCTION

▼

I am Nuit.
I am infinite space,
and the infinite stars thereof.
I am above you and in you.
My ecstasy is in yours.
My joy is to see your joy.[1]

This is a book about one of the world's oldest and most widespread religions, one that curiously enough is never mentioned among lists of the so-called major religions. Once great and encompassing, this religion seems now to be a lost creed, one that I believe has been conveniently forgotten because it is a religion that focuses on women and the Goddess, and because it is a religion that incorporates and celebrates sexuality.

Concerning the topic of religious sexuality or sexual religiosity—for some people such a challenging notion as to be an impossibility—there have been only a few works written, usually by heretics or eccentrics and circulated in limited editions among the "scientific" community. The major drawback of most of these publications is the fact that they are very much centered on the phallus, so much so that the whole field of study has become known as *phallic worship*. While several books include short entries about worship directed at the female genitals or worship that focuses on sexual union, these writers call all manner of such veneration phallic worship. Although many good books about Goddess-oriented and Earth-based religions and woman's spirituality have recently been published, a book about the veneration of the Yoni had yet, until now, to be written.

It seems only appropriate that in a time such as ours, a time when the Old Religion is being revived in various ways, there should be a work dealing solely and outspokenly with the worship of the Yoni. When Inner Traditions recently decided to publish a study of the Phallus and its role in religious history,[2] the idea was conceived to balance such a publication with a book that is entirely focused on the Yoni. Knowing me to be deeply involved with this topic and perhaps suspecting me to be an active worshiper, Inner Traditions

initiated a chain of events that led straight to the here and now in which you hold this book in your hand and read these words.

Let me invite you on a fascinating journey to the Source of All.

WHY *YONI*?

Yoni is the term I use throughout my writings and my life when referring to the female genitals. A Sanskrit word, *yoni* translates as "womb," "origin," and "source," and more specifically, "vulva." The choice to use this term rather than any from our Western languages seems to me—and to most women I know—a natural one, considering that *yoni* carries neither an undercurrent of clinical detachment, as does *vulva* or *vagina*, nor any of the pornographic, immature, and often derogatory connotations that colloquial words such as *cunt, pussy,* or similar terms do.[▾]

In contrast to these words, the term *yoni* heralds from a culture and religion in which women have long been regarded and honored as the embodiment of divine female energy—the goddess known as Shakti—and where the female genitals are seen as a sacred symbol of the Great Goddess. Because the Eastern Tantrics and other ancient cultures worship the Divine in the form of a Goddess, the term *yoni* has also acquired another, more cosmic meaning, becoming a symbol of the Universal Womb, the Matrix of Generation and Source of All.

THE YONI

[▾] For other possibilities regarding the naming of this part of a woman's body, see chapter 8 and Appendix II.

Taking all of this one step further, I prefer to use the term in an even more holistic sense. Considering that *yoni*, in its original language, can refer to both the vulva (the outer, visible aspect of the female genitals) and the womb (the innermost aspect hidden from view), I propose that *yoni* be used to denote the female genital system as a whole.

Yet there is more. If we look at the word itself and at the letters used to write it in its original language, there are several surprises in store, at least for those unacquainted with Sanskrit. To be able to value what the individual letters that compose the word *yoni* stand for, it is important to know that Sanskrit is not a language for everyday use (see glossary); it is instead a language that was consciously designed for the purpose of recording religious and ritual traditions and their content. As is also the case with ancient Hebrew and Greek, in such a sacred language each letter holds a particular meaning and a symbolic, philosophical value before and beyond the fact of its use as part of a word. Thus, the esoteric meaning or symbolism of each letter of the Sanskrit alphabet or *devanagari* (S: "language of the gods") defines the innermost content of a given word.▾

On that level, the word created by the four letters *y, o, n,* and *i* is a construction of various concepts. In devanagari, the word *yoni* is written as shown at right. The letters, read from left to right, signify the following:

Y = The animating principle, the heart, the true self, union
O = Preservation, brightness
I = Love, desire, consciousness; to shine, to pervade; pain and sorrow
N = Lotus, motherhood, menstrual cycle, nakedness, emptiness, pearl

This succession of letters is a peculiarity of Sanskrit. Although pronounced *yō-nee*, the word is written as *yoin*.

WORSHIP OF THE YONI

This much will become clear in the pages that follow: Worship of the Yoni means worship of the Goddess, and worship of woman as the Goddess's living representative. As such this book, seemingly about the most intimate, private aspect of the female anatomy, is about much more than that. In the final analysis, this is a book about women and how they have been regarded in cultures and religious systems of belief that were less patriarchal than are most contemporary ones.

There is an ongoing discussion within the scientific community regarding whether the civilizations of our ancestors were matriarchal in their organization and focus. Although this book does not specifically address that issue, it does give abundant visual and textual evidence suggesting that woman, with her intrinsic energies and her unique powers and potentials, was in civilizations past regarded as superior to man.

Whatever the scientific community may or may not believe, certain facts are beyond doubt. It was woman who was first elevated to divine status when our paleolithic ances-

---

▾ The following abreviations are used for foreign terms defined in the text: A=Arabic, C=Chinese, E=Egyptian, G=Greek, H=Hebrew, J=Japanese, L=Latin, N=Nepali, OE=Old English, S=Sanskrit, T=Tibetan.

FIGURE 7
In this rock painting from
Arnhem Land, the Australian
All Mother is shown revealing
herself to a circle of women,
imparting her teachings
concerning the female creative
powers.

tors began thinking and acting along lines that we now regard as "religious" or "spiritual." The burial rites of Neanderthal men and women show the first evidence of religious activity among humans. Their successors, the so-called Cro-Magnon wo/men who spread throughout Europe from about 35,000 B.C.E., introduced the next stage in the evolution of worship, creating sculptures, engravings, and cave paintings of Divine Woman and the Magical Yoni. Chapters 1 through 3 trace this development in detail; chapters 4 through 8 show what is left of the worship of Divine Woman, what secretly survived the male uprising during which the desire for equality—inspired by recognition of men's part in procreation—resulted in male domination of all peoples, lands, and systems, a legacy with which we still live.

At some point in history, different in time but common to all continents and most cultures, the Goddess-based religions were either destroyed or forced underground by male-oriented systems. To state it briefly here, the patriarchal religion of Jehovah was the first to destroy a Goddess-oriented religion when the leaders abolished the so-called heathen practices of worshiping the golden calf, a symbol of the Great Cow Goddess of those regions. This denouncement was to be followed several centuries later by the soldiers of Allah, who turned the Arabian people from worshipers of the Triple Goddess into followers of the One God. Similarly, invading hordes of northern Indo-Europeans achieved much the same results in India, Greece, and Crete, while Christianized Romans subjugated a range of peoples from Egypt to Ireland.

Over the span of a few millennia—and sometimes only centuries—the world was turned around, and male deities, such as the notorious Greek god Zeus, assumed power. With Zeus came heavily armed troops and newly installed priests to enforce his directives. By rewriting history and mythology, the male leaders established themselves as rulers. Their myths sometimes even claimed that males were able to create—to actually give birth—betraying the fact that this ability was their great envy.

How absurd it is that our present-day cultures are based on a belief that women are the "lesser" or "weaker" of the two sexes. How absolutely ignorant—or perhaps even insane—is the Freudian notion that women should have ever suffered from penis envy when in fact the human male seems rather to be suffering from yoni envy.

This book shows convincing evidence that woman and her Yoni have been worshiped, openly or in secret, since the beginning of humanity, and that such worship continues to the present day. "Today?" you may ask, with justified disbelief. "Tell me where." Yes, even today, and in countries where women at large are often treated with more disdain than in the rest of the world. For example, in India and Bangladesh there exist certain secret schools where woman, the Goddess, and the Yoni are honored not only (as it is so

FIGURE 8
Seldom does one encounter so honest an emblem of sheer and unadulterated patriarchy as in this Roman bas-relief from Nimes, France.

FIGURE 9
Several examples of yoni symbology have been found in the prehistoric caves of southern Europe. These carvings are from the Moigny cave on the Île-de-France.

FIGURE 10
A classical example of the male desire to imitate female powers. In this alchemical emblem, the Greek god Zeus gives birth to Pallas Athena, with the divine smith Hephaestos assuming the role of midwife. Typically, this birth originated in the head, and the goddess thus birthed was to become a goddess of war.

easily interpreted) for the powers of fertility, but even more so for menstruation and for the energies associated with female sexuality.

In a time such as ours, a time in which there is a great need for positive role models on which women, young and old, can draw in their search for a true identity beyond those imposed by patriarchal systems, it is important to know how women have been revered through the ages. Woman is not a singular archetype, although we often speak or write as if such a woman does indeed exist. Instead, woman manifests in thousands of uniquely individual ways; and so it is that we need many more and different role models than have as yet been provided by such best-selling authors as Jean Shinoda Bolen,[3] Merlin Stone,[4] and others. In this book we will encounter archetypes of women from ancient Greece to medieval Tibet and from ancient Japan to present-day India who were and are deeply aware of their unique sexual powers, free from shame about their bodies and their sexuality. Such women have been leaders and priestesses, regarded by their communities as important teachers and high initiates.

Naturally, such roles are not desired or wanted by all women, and that too is valid. However, in a time when "political correctness" requires that one deny sexuality as something important, something to fully explore and celebrate, role models of deeply embodied sexuality are seldom discussed, except perhaps in the context of what is known as sacred prostitution. It is my hope that the information on Yoni worship and the models of spiritually rich and sexually expressive women presented in this book will prove inspiring to you.

▼

1

DEEP ROOTS

The Mother of songs, the mother of our whole seed, bore us in the beginning. She is the mother of all races of men and the mother of all tribes. She is the mother of thunder, of rivers, of trees and all kinds of things. She is the mother of the dance paraphernalia and of all temples, and the only mother we have. She is the mother of the animals, the only one, and the mother of the Milky Way. She is the mother of rain, the only one we have. She alone is the mother of things, she alone.

FROM A SONG OF THE KAGABA INDIANS, COLUMBIA[1]

However convinced some writers may be about how our earliest human ancestors lived and worshiped, we should always remind ourselves that we will never actually *know* the answer to such inquiries. We can guess; we can even make informed guesses. We can try to imagine. We can gather different kinds of data to serve as pieces of a large and complicated puzzle. But we cannot and will not *know* for certain what exactly transpired in the history of early humanity. We do not know how our ancestors lived; we do not know what they thought and felt, what they experienced and suffered, what they envisioned and dreamed of.

When reading fiction we know from the be-ginning that we are in the realm of fantasy, and therefore we do not readily trick ourselves into regarding what is written to be factual. In the case of nonfiction writing, however, it is often quite difficult to separate actual fact from the author's personal conclusions, to in essence discern the fictional content of a "scientific" work.

The conclusion of a scientific study may be the result of the author's/reaseacher's best intentions. At other times, though, such conclusions may be consciously put forth and validated in order to promote the author's or researcher's political and moral views. Conclusions drawn in the latter case are a nuisance at best and outright dangerous at worst. Convinced and fearful patriarchists—or, for that matter, overzealous feminists—who more or less elegantly play down, dismiss, or altogether ignore unsuitable evidence remake the world in their own image. Whether or not it is consciously disseminated, such disinformation has resulted in a collective image of human history that is not only incomplete but also slanted toward the concept that male domination is a natural state of human affairs.

Even more damaging to our sense of cultural history are moralist authors of whatever faith. All too often such writers judge a certain behavior or a particular image as rude, indecent, obscene, or immoral by their own contemporary rules or convictions. This is especially true with a subject such as sexuality. It is ironic that the same behavior or image that evokes such ire in the present is (or was) most likely sanctioned by the culture(s) being written about, is (was), on a more personal level, completely free of shame or guilt. Any behavior regarded as obscene today leads some authors to conclude that "those people" of earlier epochs simply had no morals. It is important to realize that the true moralist is always a fundamentalist: it is simply not possible for him or her to understand the existence of varying moral constructs, or to recognize that the concepts of decency and obscenity not only are relative but may not have even existed in many earlier cultures.

THE EARLIEST GODDESSES

Ever since Erich Neumann attempted to elucidate the subject of the Goddess in his book *The Great Mother*, published in 1955, and especially since Merlin Stone's pioneering *Paradise Papers*, published in 1978, a constant flow of writings, lectures, and workshops aimed at reclaiming the Goddess has entered the stream of our cultural consciousness. As a result, there are few people in the literate world today who have not yet seen a reproduction of the most famous of all ancient female statues, the Venus of Willendorf, supposedly the oldest of all sculptures ever made by a paleolithic artist. It may come as a surprise to know that such a Venus never existed and does not exist today, and we will soon see why.

It is a great pity that this sculpture, and many similar figures created after her, were given the name Venus. In the absence of written records, of course, no one could have known the names of these sculptures: the particular statue in question predates writing by at least twenty thousand years. Nevertheless, it would have served both her and us better if she had been found by a more knowledgeable, open-minded, and visionary man or woman who would perhaps have named her Ancient Earth Mother, Mother of Old Europe, or even Great Goddess of southeastern Europe. Her name seems to have been given to her simply because the Roman Venus was one of the few female deities popularly known at the time of the statue's discovery in 1908. Actually, in comparison with the Roman goddess, the Venus discussed here is no Venus at all. Not, as some cynical authors keep insisting, because her body is full, heavy, and round as opposed to the male-invented ideal of slender beauty and attractiveness one recognizes in images of the Roman Venus. The statue from Willendorf is no Venus simply because her image is so much more pow-

FIGURE 12
Almost 30,000 years after
an unknown artist created
the powerful Doni of
Willendorf, contemporary
artists are still inspired by
this ancient masterpiece. One
such modern copy of the
original is this bronze by
Dutch silversmith Nicky
Oosterbaan.

FIGURE 13
Venus, the classical Roman
goddess of femininity, is
clearly no match for the
female prowess symbolized by
the Great Mother of All.

erful and her ranking and importance so much higher than that of the Roman goddess of love and beauty.[*]

There is, in fact, no such deity as the Venus of Willendorf, a title that suggests to a modern mind that she had some connection with a (at the time nonexistent) geopolitical entity called Austria. What I observe when I see representations of the statue of Willendorf is a truly archetypal representation of all the later concepts variously known as Great Goddess, Creatrix, Great Mother, Life Giver, Earth Mother, or—as in the song of the Kagaba Indians—the Mother of our Whole Seed.

The creation of this statue of Doni[**] has been estimated at somewhere around 27,500 B.C.E. Her status as the oldest of all goddess sculptures was apparently lost in 1988 with the discovery of the statue that has been called the Dancing Venus of Galgenberg

---

[*] Venus herself was merely a degenerated version of the Near Eastern and Greek Aphrodite.

[**] Considering that many of the oldest known and preserved works of art—religious in nature and depicting woman, the Goddess, and the Yoni—come from Old Europe (a geographical term introduced by Marija Gimbutas [see bibliography]) and especially from the vast regions along the Danube river (also known as the Danu or Donau), I prefer to call the oldest representations of the Goddess not Venus figurines but simply Mother or sometimes Doni, based on the names Danube, Donau, and Danu and on the Yoni, her ultimate symbol and the place of her power.

Deep Roots

(as it was then, the Venus misunderstanding is still alive), one that dates back to approximately 30,000 B.C.E. Although this particular figure was also found in present-day Austria, Goddess artifacts of similar antiquity have also been found in the region that ranges from present-day Spain and France, via Austria, Italy, and the former Czechoslovakia, to Russia and the Ukraine.

The following timeline lists and describes the most important representations of the ancient Great Mother found in this region to date, making it clear that the Goddess as a symbol of female power had a wide following throughout the whole of southern and eastern Europe. This timeline represents an overview of prehistoric artifacts that apparently stem from a cultural substratum in which all attention and reverence was directed at women, the Yoni, and the Goddess.

40,000—30,000 B.C.E.

♦ Artwork from this period has yet to be found. If we do not discover such items, it does not mean that no such art was ever produced; it may simply mean that less durable materials were used in their making. Anything made out of materials other than bone or stone—wood, fur, or leather, for example—will disintegrate over time and eventually perish.

30,000—25,000 B.C.E.

♦ The very oldest of all known depictions of the Goddess or the specifically female powers of women are the rock-incised triangles and other depictions of the Yoni found in many of the now French caves such as La Ferrassie, Abri Blanchard, Castanet, Cellier, Laussel, Poisson, Les Rois, and others. Some of these date back to 30,000 B.C.E., others to 28,000 B.C.E. They are usually believed to be of early Aurignacian origin, but some may in fact have been crafted by *Homo neanderthalensis*. Both classifications of early humans seem to have used the same caves as natural shelters and places of worship.

◆ The Dancing Priestess (30,000 B.C.E.), discovered in 1988 at Galgenberg in present-day Austria, is unique among all other known figurines from this period in that she is dynamic rather than static in form. Although she is nude, with breasts that are carefully sculpted, her pose does not invite immediate associations with fertility. The figure most likely depicts an inspired shamaness going into trance before a gathering of her tribe.

FIGURE 15
In these 30,000-year-old rock incisions from La Ferrassie, one can get a sense of how lovingly and laboriously such yoni symbols were carved into the stone.

◆ The Doni of Willendorf (27,800 B.C.E.), probably the best-known work of prehistoric art, is a corpulent limestone figure 11 cm high, with arms resting on her huge breasts. Discovered in 1908 on the river Danube near Vienna, Austria, the ivory-colored figure was covered with red ochre, a sacred substance regarded by many peoples as the blood of the Earth.

◆ The so-called vulva rocks from Kostenki (25,000 B.C.E.), a shrine discovered in 1932 at Kostenki, 500 km south of Moscow at the river Don, has yielded a number of rock medallions similar to the incised yonis of the cave artists in present-day France. The same site also contained several female figurines named the Mothers of Kostenki.

◆ The Doni of Lespugue (27,000–23,000 B.C.E.), a beautiful masterpiece, was found

Figure 16
The famous Doni of Laussel, a
26,000-year-old limestone
relief found in France. In her
hand she holds the archetypal
model of what later became
known as the "horn of plenty"
or the infamous "box of
Pandora."

in the region that is now Haute-Garonne in southern France. This goddess figurine is elegantly stylized, with the attention focused on her huge belly and buttocks and her even more extravagant breasts.

25,000—20,000 B.C.E.

◆ The Goddess of Savignano (29,000—20,000 B.C.E.) is a very stylized, almost abstract figure from a site in present-day northern Italy.

◆ The Doni of Laussel (24,000 B.C.E.) is a limestone relief (46 cm) hewn into a cave wall. The site of Laussel is southeast of Perigueux, Dordogne, in present-day France. Besides the usual corpulence and large breasts, this goddess holds a moon-shaped horn (likely a mammoth's tusk) in her right hand. This symbol is one that is encountered across time, appearing millennia later in myths and depictions of other peoples. Resting on her belly, the goddess's other hand seems to point at her Yoni.▼

◆ The Mother of Dolni Vestonice (23,650 B.C.E.), a statuette made from a mixture of

▼ This was first recognized by female artist and author W. M. Lubell.

powdered bone and clay, was found near Mikulov in the former Czechoslovakia. Another sample from this site is a small head, possibly the oldest sculpture with clearly defined facial features.

- The Mothers of Grimaldi are two female figures found in the caves of Grimaldi near what is now the French/Italian border. One is a corpulent figure similar to the statue from Willendorf; the second figure is quite obviously pregnant.

- The Goddess of Menton, found at a site near Grimaldi, is a small limestone sculpture that almost looks like a copy of the Goddess of Willendorf, except for showing a figure less heavy in the belly and breasts.

- The Doni of Gagarino, a figure cut from mammoth ivory, is quite similar to the figures from Willendorf and Grimaldi. This Doni was found in Gagarino, 280 km south of Moscow, near the source of the river Don.

20,000—15,000 B.C.E.

This period, the height of the last glaciation, was a time during which human survival was most difficult. Still, or perhaps therefore, the craftsmen and artists of this period took the time to create many images of woman or the Goddess.

- The Mothers of Buret' and Mal'ta (c. 18,000 B.C.E.) are highly stylized figurines from two sites 100 km northwest of Irkutsk in what is now Russia. At Mal'ta, a surprisingly large number of small statues (twenty) have been found, all carved in mammoth ivory and ranging from 3 to 13 cm in size. One of these seems to be clothed in the fur of a cave lion; the others are naked.

- The Goddess of Predmosti, a deity engraved on a rod of mammoth ivory, is from a site in the former Czechoslovakia.

- The Lady of Brassempouy is a small (3.2 cm) ivory head found at the Grotte du Pape at Brassempouy, presently southern France. It is quite different from most other figures of this period in that it is one of the two oldest-known carvings daring to depict a specific individual by representing a human face.

15,000—10,000 B.C.E.

- Magdalenian cave paintings found at Lascaux (15,000 B.C.E.), in what is present-day Dordogne, France.

- Symbols of the Yoni (14,000 B.C.E.) found in the cave of El Castillo, near Santander in present-day Spain.

- Symbols of the Yoni found in the Moigny cave, Île-de-France, in present-day France (see page 5, figure 9).

- The Doni of La Madeleine, a rock engraving of a sleeping or leisurely resting goddess found in the caves at La Madeleine, present-day France. The artistic presentation shows an advancement in sensitivity as well as in perspective.

- The ancient Triple Goddess, three rock-engraved nudes found at Angles sur-l'Anglin in present-day France.

- The cave paintings at Altamira (12,000 B.C.E.), in what is now northern Spain.

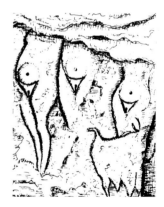

FIGURE 17
A truly ancient version (c. 15,000—10,000 B.C.E.) of the triple goddesses found in the much later religions of Europe and the Near East. By showing the yoni together with the moon's three phases, the Paleolithic artists demonstrate their awareness of the menstrual cycle.

Deep Roots

FIGURE 18
Female imagery clearly
dominates all sacred art in the
ancient caves, as it does in these
wall paintings of three vulvas
from 14,000 B.C.E. in the cave of
El Castillo in Spain.

It is important to recognize that not one single work of sacred art existent from this thirty-thousand-year period shows a sculptural representation of a male. We have found various male symbols, male animals, and male hunters in European cave art, including the famous ithyphallic figure from the cave at Lascaux, but that is all. Not a single sculpture has been found—no minutely carved figurines, no carefully chiseled statues. Does this say anything about the status of women among our ancestors? It surely must, even if numerous (yet not all) male historians and social analysts of past and present day still deny it.

YONI MAGIC

Although the worship of both female and male genitals is probably the original starting point of most religions, cults, and sacred customs, it is phallic worship that has been extensively studied and thus is much better known than yoni worship. However, archeological evidence points convincingly to the conclusion that the Yoni preceded the Lingam (S: phallus) as a sacred symbol and an object of veneration. Yet even without the evidence that has come to us by way of paleolithic and neolithic remains of sacred art, the conclusion regarding the primacy of Yoni worship can be arrived at by a completely different approach, at least to everyone with an open mind and some information about early humanity.

That the Yoni was the first to be recognized as having immense magical powers and importance can easily be understood by looking at certain aspects of life known to our earliest ancestors. One of these is the simple fact that, as now, only women were able to bring new life into the world. In the absence of hospitals, where the bloody physical reality of a woman giving birth is hidden under multiple white sheets and green cloaks, birth took place in the open and was seen by many. Truly everyone of a human tribe saw—and thus knew—how a future clan mother, hunter, shamaness, or warrior came into being: out of the mother's dilating Yoni, accompanied by the mother's blood and still visibly connected to her body.

Another important consideration in acknowledging the precedence the Yoni took over the lingam or phallus is more difficult to absorb. Although some may find this difficult to imagine and hard to accept, it is important to recognize that early humanity was not aware of male involvement in the process of conception and procreation. How, one may ask, can our early ancestors *not* have known about sexual reproduction, especially given the fact that they lived in close contact with the animals? How could they *not* have known, especially if the birthing and menstruation cycles were seen by all?

In order to understand the situation properly, we have to bear several things in mind. The first of these is the fact that humans are completely different from all other animals in their activities related to sexuality and fertility. The difference lies in the fact that humans clearly have no given mating season; receptivity and fertility are not governed by the estrous cycle. With the exception of some close relatives among the primates, the human female is unique in this sense; almost equally unique is the length of time that passes between conception and birth. Whereas all the animals observed by early humans followed a clearly defined pattern—seasons during which mating occurred, resulting in the birth of offspring shortly thereafter—there was no such pattern in the case of humans. Fertile year-round, women seemed to simply create whenever they or some divine agency—that is, the Goddess—deemed it should happen.

And then there was the matter of menstruation, something else that was not shared with the animals. To our ancestors, bleeding was something that occurred only if some-

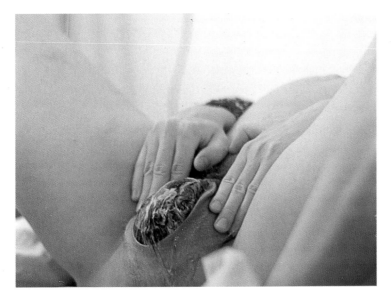

Figure 19
The yoni in action at the awesome
moment of birth, a fact of life most of
us unfortunately do not witness and
therefore do not actually know.

Deep Roots

one was wounded, and it was observed to lead to either disease or death. Imagine, then, how awed early humans must have been by the monthly menstruation. Blood flowing freely yet without dire consequences; blood flowing more or less painlessly, except for those times when a woman was visibly producing new life. It is no great wonder that our ancestors spawned the idea that women created their children from and out of that very blood—pure and awesome magic! ▾

Looking at it this way, we can more easily understand why women in some cultures spread this magical menstrual blood on the fields in order to make them fruitful, and why other cultures took to fearing the potency of that same blood so much that they excluded menstruating women from a number of daily activities.

Still, the fact that humanity should not have known about male fertility, about sperm and seed, remains a mental obstacle to many. Indeed, there are those who simply deny this possibility and therefore deny that there would have been any reason for the magical and religious awe with which woman and her Yoni have been regarded in early history and throughout time. To such people, be they scientists (who should know better) or lay-men, I would like to introduce data collected by Reay Tannahill and published in his book *Sex in History.*

According to this well-researched account, "there have been tribal peoples, even in the twentieth century, whose ignorance remains profound."[2] This statement refers specifically to the Bellonese people of the Solomon Islands (Oceania) who told Christian missionaries arriving there in the 1930s that children were sent by ancestral deities. To them, sexual intercourse was an activity that was very pleasurable yet completely unrelated to fertility. Another beautiful example of such biological "ignorance" comes from a tribal woman in twentieth-century Australia. When the Western view of conception was explained to her, indicating the man as having a contributing function, she simply and angrily replied: "Him, nothing!" Tannahill found tribal people in north Queensland in the 1960s who believed that "a woman became pregnant because she had been sitting over a fire on which she had roasted a fish given to her by the prospective father."[3] Others even believed that a man could become pregnant by eating a possum; such men, however, always died before childbirth. ▾▾ While such investigations of contemporary tribal peoples substantiate that humanity has not always known all the "facts of life," we need not look with arrogance at people who simply never had the chance to gain our precise biological and medical knowledge.

In the midst of more "advanced" cultures, children and adults are often willfully denied specific knowledge concerning sexuality, and grave ignorance can thus occur. Once

---

▾ The basic concept of the prehistoric and ancient worlds was that humans are made from the blood of woman; it is perhaps not shocking, then, to suggest that the biblical Adam carries a name that seems to be modeled on the ancient Chaldean goddess Adamu. This goddess, whose name in Chaldean means "red," was regarded as the female principle of matter; she was especially associated with menstrual blood. The biblical story of creation, written in the time when patriarchal systems were already in place, simply twisted this idea to make it appear as if woman was made of man.

▾▾ Eating the local possum resulted in a swollen stomach and was usually fatal.

again Tannahill provides us with a few surprising cases, these reported in the *London Times* on October 2, 1977:

> In modern, media-saturated England in 1977, a girl who had borne a child to a black lover wrote to the agony column of a leading women's magazine. She was about to be married to a white man; would the Negro blood still inside her mean that she would continue to have black babies? Another correspondent asked whether the Pill would save her from becoming pregnant by her lover as well as by her husband. And men, it appears, take the Pill as their wives and girl friends do, "just to be on the safe side."

WORSHIP OF THE GODDESS AMONG OUR ANCESTORS

Just how strongly paleolithic worship was centered on women and the Great Mother becomes abundantly clear when the art and symbology found in the many caves of southwestern Europe are analyzed fully, objectively, and intelligently. French scientist André Leroi-Gourhan has made just such a comprehensive study. After comparing sixty-two caves and 865 subjects therein—including artistic renderings of animals, people, hands, and vulvas—he reports that 80 percent of all female symbology occurs in a central location in the cave, whereas 88 percent of all male symbology is found on the periphery, in places such as the entrance and the tunnels.[4] On the basis of this study, Leroi-Gourhan concludes that within an "ideal paleolithic sanctuary" not only are the Yoni and other female symbols of central importance, but there is also a specific room apparently for the purpose of worshiping women and the Goddess. He suggests that the magical, religious, and ritual life of our paleolithic ancestors seems to have called for a sacred room dedicated exclusively to the Yoni and those the Yoni symbolized.

One clear example of such a sacred room is found in the extensive subterranean system of Tito Bustillo, a cave in present-day Ribadesella, Asturies, Spain. Leroi-Gourhan describes a small, separate room as the "Gallery of the Vulvas"[5] that sits at the far end of this cave, about 350 meters from the entrance. Figure 20 shows not only the general layout of the cave with the room under discussion at the far right, but also the four different Yonis that have been painted on the walls.

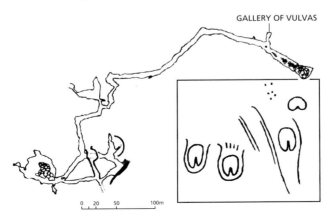

GALLERY OF VULVAS

Figure 20
The existence in some caves of a chamber marked solely with vulvas indicates that the people using these caves had specific rituals concerning women, the Goddess, and the yoni. In the cave at Tito Bustillo in Spain, the chamber of vulvas was located deep within the system, shown in the small diverticulum on the top right of this figure.

Deep Roots

FIGURE 21
An 8,000-year-old-sculpture from Lepenski Vir in former Yugoslavia. The design very much resembles those created by Goddess-worshiping artisans 20,000 years ago in the caves of France and Spain, evidencing an unbroken tradition of yoni worship.

Considering all of the above, we can be certain that women, at least those who held the office of clan mother, shamaness, or priestess, were considered in high regard and took a central place in worship. It is also certain that the power they were seen to possess, the "magic" they were able to produce, was strongly related to the Yoni and its unique ability to bleed in cycles with the moon (menstruation) and to give birth to new life (fertility). In the absence of written records, what will remain forever unknown is the exact nature of the rituals and the beliefs held by these early ancestors. However, the evidence gathered from the disciplines of anthropology, ethnology, and comparative religious studies discussed in this book suggests that these rituals were most likely coming-of-age initiations (for girls having their menarche), defloration ceremonies, sexual initiations, and various celebrations accompanying birth and menstruation cycles.

The gifted artisans among our ancestors, a people heartily challenged to survive the daily hardships of life, set aside considerable time and energy to create paintings and sculptures celebrating life through the images of the Goddess and the Yoni. As we will see in the chapter that follows, they also clearly noticed and appreciated any natural object that had the shape of the Yoni. To our ancestors, these were reminders of the Goddess's presence in all things. Where many people today see something "obscene," our ancestors saw the ten thousand Yonis of Mother Earth.

2

THE TEN THOUSAND YONIS OF MOTHER EARTH

*The mons veneris of the Mother
is the triangle of Aphrodite,
the "mound of Venus," the mountain connecting
man and woman, earth and sky.*[1]

Across all times and places, humans have taken notice of countless natural shapes that resemble the Yoni. Inevitably such natural occurrences—be they canyons, craters, cave entrances, flowers, fruits, or shells—were declared sacred by worshipers of the Goddess; often the locations of large or truly unique objects became places of pilgrimage. In this chapter we will examine a variety of such naturally occurring symbols, as well as some artifacts and monuments that, though created by human hands, bear striking resemblance to the expressions of nature. Through that investigation it will become clear that the number 10,000 in reference to manifestations of Mother Earth's Yoni is no empty claim. It is more likely a rather conservative estimate of the many ways, large and small, in which Mother Earth displays her Yoni to those who honor her.▼

It seems that where such natural symbols were lacking, especially on a larger scale, our ancestors were ever ready to give nature a hand. In the same way that Zen monks arrange their truly natural-looking gardens in beautiful and altogether predetermined ways, so did worshipers of the Mother create overgrown,

▼ In early Chinese philosophy, the number 10,000 did not imply an accurate count but was instead used as a symbolic figure to denote "innumerable." The expression "ten thousand things" refers to a multitude that is impossible to count.

FIGURE 23
The "lips" of this natural rock
formation in the southern
California desert were painted
before the site was used for
initiation ceremonies for the girls
and women of the indigenous
Kemeyaay tribe.

megalithic Yonis, enhancing cave entrances with chisel and color, building Yoni-shaped tombs, or scratching a meaningful cleft into suitable pebbles.

Among the sacred sites connected to Yoni worship are shrines that were built within caves or around sacred stones or were constructed to represent the female and male forces of life and the universe. Many such places of personal and communal worship, such as the Yonimandala of Assam, the holy Kaaba at Mecca, and any of the dolmens of Europe and India, are places where the Yoni was—and still is—prayed to and venerated. Sometimes the sacred yonic symbol is kissed or touched; sometimes it is drunk from or lain in.

Other sites, such as ring stones, are seminatural constructions. Starting with a large rock that contained an already sizeable hole (perhaps from water erosion), Yoni worshipers would enlarge the hole to a size that allowed a human to pass through. Such stones thus became sites for fertility rituals or served as a gate of initiation: by passing through this Yoni, the initiate would be reborn.

Though on a much smaller scale, any small stone with a hole in it was also seen as a no less important symbol of the Yoni. On finding such a stone, a male follower of the Goddess would test whether or not this objet trouvé would fit his lingam. If it did, he would have the object consecrated and would proudly carry it as an amulet. There was little doubt to our ancestors that finding such an object had clear spiritual and magical significance; the Yoni object was laid on their path by divine intervention. The concept of coincidence simply did not exist. All and everything was seen as ruled, fated, or at least meaningful, and of divine or supernatural origin. This so-called magical consciousness has as a fundamental tenet something akin to the Jungian concept of synchronicity, a modern way of understanding meaningful or auspicious coincidences. Finding any object that looked similar to a Yoni was a truly auspicious and Goddess-given synchronicity. It was considered a sign and a portent—a message from the divine realms to the human.

CRATERS AND CANYONS, ROCKS AND TOMBS

Figures 23 and 24 show natural rock formations known to have been used as places of worship and initiation by Native American tribes. Knowing that the early inhabitants of what is now the United States used such natural formations in this way, we can readily imagine that the same kinds of rituals happened in other lands, even if our historians do not have convincing evidence of such. Simply imagine how it would feel to a worshiper of the Goddess and her Yoni when she or he first encountered the large and undeniably Yoni-like crater in what is now Tongariro National Park in New Zealand (page vi), or the beautiful and serene Yoni-shaped canyon of the Colorado River shown on page 22. Awed by the sight, such a person would spread the story of this discovery among all he

FIGURE 24
Another natural rock formation used as a place of worship in the United States. This one can be found on the Crawford Ranch in California's San Diego County.

Ten Thousand Yonis

or she met along the way, and certainly to everyone back home. Depending on the distance and the hardship involved in traveling there, many people of the tribe—if not all—would travel there together in order to see once more the wonder that is the Great Mother.

And do we guess wrong if we assume that something similar happened to the people of Thailand—where even money was once Yoni shaped—when they first encountered the unmistakable Yoni in the cliffs of Koh Samui? Here, between what looks like huge, open legs, waves from the sea continuously wash over and into the Yoni known as Grandmother's Stone by the local people. Nearby stands Grandfather's Stone, this one in the form of a huge phallus.

Whether or not these stones are natural formations or were artificially erected or enhanced remains a mystery. However, we do know that people of many eras and cultures often built huge and difficult-to-construct objects specifically created to resemble the Goddess's Yoni. Foremost among all man-made sacred sites, certainly in regard to size but also in regard to being the most well known, are the megaliths (G: "great stones"). To most people, the term *megaliths* immediately conjures up images of Stonehenge (England), Carnac (France), or temples of the Great Goddess such as Hagiar Kim and others on the

FIGURE 25
A place of mystery and stillness, but not of solitude. To the worshiper, the Goddess resides in such natural formations that reveal the Yoni of Mother Earth.

FIGURE 26 (LEFT)
Hin Yaay, a formation in the cliffs of the Thai island of Koh Samui. In local parlance it is called Grandmother's Stone.

FIGURE 27 (BELOW)
This megalithic monument in Kerala, India, is an almost exact look-a-like to the dolmens of Celtic Europe, testifying to an archetypal Yoni symbolism that crosses all cultural and linguistic boundaries.

Maltese Islands. These and uncounted other megaliths of England, Scotland, Wales, France, Germany, and those found throughout southern Europe, all remainders of Celtic and pre-Celtic cultures and religions, have so dominated contemporary consciousness that those of other early societies are rather forgotten. However, megalithic monuments are also to be found in India, Egypt, the Indonesian Islands, and South America. Such monuments are known as dolmen (female) and menhir (male). Though their use and function may not have been entirely sexual, this certainly played a great part in the motivation for erecting and building them. Their locations often coincide with subterranean waterways or other energy currents in the earth, and the stones themselves may have been placed to heal energetic disturbances or to amplify the subtle energies naturally available at these places.

Translating as "stone table," *dolmen* is a Celtic word that describes a large, horizontal slab of stone resting on two or more vertical stones. Symbolizing the Yoni as the female womb-gate, the dolmen is associated with the powers of birth and rebirth, and as such also with the beyond. One of the most interesting dolmens is that of Crucuno (near Carnac, France), where, during the autumnal equinox, the incoming sunlight creates a downward-pointing triangle, a well-known symbol of the Yoni (see figure 28). In centuries past, young girls would lie naked on such "hot stones" in order to find the hunter, craftsman, or tribal leader of their fantasies, or in order to conceive the child of their dreams. Even as recently as 1989, as reported by the German magazine *Esotera,* some French women sat upon such dolmens in order to enhance their fertility. Similar megalithic arrangements have also been found in India.

FIGURE 28
At the dolmen of Crucuno (near Carnac, France) the rays of the sun generate a Yoni shape at the exact moment of the autumnal equinox, a result that was both intended and astronomically calculated by its early builders.

Ten Thousand Yonis

Sometimes, however, as we can see in figure 29, the symbol and form of the Yoni was not only one of life and birth but one of death as well. To many peoples the Great Mother, the Giver of Life, the Earth herself was also responsible for taking her children back into her womb. To a worshiper of the Mother who was a person of high esteem, a special yoni-shaped tomb was fashioned after the Mother's womb. For most others, the Earth herself became the place where the dead body was laid to rest for the long sleep in her womb. Ever since Neanderthal▾ and Cro-Magnon humans settled in what is now Europe, such burial rites were clearly meant to reflect birth; people left life just as they entered it. It seems that in their burial rites our early ancestors, as well as tribal people of the nineteenth and twentieth centuries, often used red ochre, a sacred substance regarded as the blood of the Earth. As the birthing journey was accompanied by blood, so was the transition of death.

Meteorites, those suddenly appearing stones that fell from the heavens and as such were seemingly sent by divine forces, were also considered to be sacred objects. Probably the most famous meteorite honored as representing the Divine is the famous Black Stone at Mecca, still visited by millions of pilgrims annually.

Many peoples across time have been fascinated by the beauty and power of such heaven-sent stones, and have worshiped these stones either as deities themselves or as representatives of a deity dwelling in the stone. Often these chunks of stone were protected in a special building that was jealously guarded by selected warriors. The Black Stone at Mecca seems to have originally been revered as the Yoni of the Arabian goddess Al'Lat (see page 50). Goddesses of other cultures and religious beliefs are also known to have been associated with white or black chunks of meteoritic stones.▾▾ Often the stones were sacred objects in and of themselves; sometimes the stone was formed into the shape of the Goddess or the Yoni. To name but a few such sacred sites in Europe and the Near East, we may mention the sanctuary of the goddess Aphrodite at Paphos, the temple of Cybele at Pessinus and later in Rome, or the temple to Astarte at Byblos. Last but not least, there was the famous Ephesian Artemis (sometimes falsely called Diana) whose most ancient sculpture had been cut from a black meteorite. This goddess irritated Saint Paul so much that his fulminations against her as written in the Bible made her more famous than other goddesses for whom we have no literary evidence.

FLOWERS, FRUITS, NUTS, SEEDS, AND SHELLS

It seems only obvious that huge canyons, large craters, or big boulders would speak more strongly to the imagination than a small shell or blossom. Yet, naturally occurring Yoni symbols are more abundant in the realm of organic life than in the mineral kingdom, and so it is that people of many cultures found fascination with all kinds of living things that bore the Goddess's imprint. The Goddess lives and manifests herself in the shapes of

FIGURE 29
Norn's Tump (above) and Windmill Tumb (below) are two examples of Neolithic long barrows that were used as tombs. Often, as in these figures, the entrance to the tomb was shaped like a vulva. Clearly the intention was to return the dead to the Great Mother from whence they came.

▾ It was the Neanderthal people who actually "invented" burials, a step that may be regarded as the first expression of a religious view of the world.

▾▾ Once inside earth's atmosphere, white meteorites often turn black. This explains why historical accounts describe white stones that today are black.

many plants, shells, fruits, nuts, and seeds that often resemble—some distinctly, some vaguely—the female genitals.

Our ancestors recognized the sacred symbol of the universal feminine in the shapes of cowrie and scallop shells; in flowers such as the lotus, lily, and rose; in fruits like the apricot, fig, and the unique *coco-de-mer*; or even in the tiny seeds of the cardamom. Humans of all millennia attached mythical and religious meaning to such flowers, fruits, or shells; sometimes their spiritual value was translated into the material realm as well, as happened to the cowrie shell that was used as currency in Asia and Africa. These gifts from nature, under whatever name and in whatever manifestation or guise, were regarded as symbolic representations of the Great Goddess. As such, each of these symbols also represented woman and her yin essence, the creative force without which there would be no life at all.

Because of their shape at a particular stage of growth, there are several flowers and plants that qualify as symbols of the Yoni. The lotus flower, a type of water lily, is regarded in India as a symbol representing transformation and unfoldment as well as purity and fertility. Its Sanskrit name, *padma*, is not only an alternative name for the goddess Lakshmi but also a code word for the Yoni of either Goddess or woman. Lotus symbolism in India is widespread, and in Indian myths we find several goddesses who are clearly connected with the symbolism of the lotus as Yoni.▾ The lotus flower was held equally sacred by the Egyptian, Persian, and Japanese cultures, though sometimes with a different symbology.

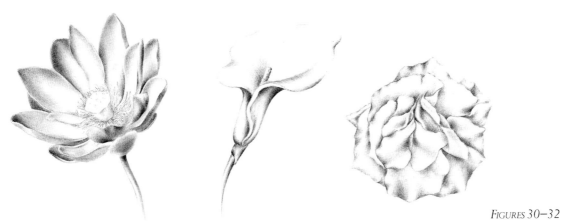

Lilies in general are flowers often used to symbolize the Yoni; this flower is also seen as a symbol of female/male union. The lily was especially popular in Middle Eastern and Mediterranean cultures. In addition to symbolizing the Yoni, love, and passion, the lily can also signify one particular aspect of woman, that of the physical virgin. Specific goddesses with whom the lily is associated are Aphrodite, Lilith, Eostre, and Juno.

The symbol of the rose is to the Occidental world what the lotus is to the cultures of Asia and the Middle East—a foremost feminine, mystic, and sacred symbol, open to diverse interpretations and usages. Sacred to the Greek goddess Aurora and the Roman

▾ Among these goddesses are Amrita, Brahmani, Kamakhya (see chapter 4), Kamala, and Lakshmi. Any complete work on Indian mythology will feature their stories.

Figures 30–32
These three drawings by Christina Camphausen show the major flowers that symbolize the Yoni in a variety of cultures (from left to right): the lotus, the lily, and the rose.

Ten Thousand Yonis

FIGURE 33
In this painting, Dutch artist Vincent Dame takes the linguistic equation "plum equals vulva" to its visually realistic conclusion.

Venus, the rose has become a foremost symbol of love and joy, desire and beauty. In rituals honoring the Egyptian Isis and the Christian Mary, however, the rose stands for chastity, virginity, and those types of love free of carnal associations. It is interesting to note that the Virgin Mary is sometimes called Mystic Rose, an appellation that is found in the writings of Rosicrucians, Qabbalists, and alchemists. Sometimes the texts of the two latter groups use this term as code for the Yoni.

Apart from these well-known flowers, a number of plants or their fruits have become associated with the Yoni. The myrtle, for example, a plant sacred to the goddess Aphrodite, was used by the Greek physician Rufus of Ephesus (first century) to name the lips of a woman's Yoni. He called the labia majora "lips of the myrtle" and the labia minora "fruit of the myrtle." The leaves of the willow were considered symbols of the Yoni by the Manchu peoples of precommunist China, the leaves likely representing the Yoni of the goddess Fuduo Mama (Manchu: Mother Willow Branch). Phrygian mythology maintains that the almond originally sprang from the Yoni of Cybele, a goddess venerated all over the Middle East and along the Mediterranean coast. This almond/yoni association is especially interesting when we note that the shape of the almond parallels that of the abstract, mathematically constructed *vesica piscis*, a shape of perfection in sacred geometry and one that is sometimes used as background in the iconography of Mary, the mother of Christ. In such paintings, Mary—with the Divine Child in her arms or suckling at her breast—often stands in the center of an almond-shaped mandorla (see page 31), secretly representing the Divine Yoni, the Source of All.

Several fruits, nuts, and seeds have become associated with the Yoni simply because of their general shape. Among these are the deeply clefted figs and apricots, as well as the plum and the peach.[*] The latter is perhaps better known for its association in Chinese culture with youthfulness and immortality, as found in the myths of Kuan-yin and in the Chinese expression "peach juice of immortality." However, as a popular type of peach found in China is an especially deeply clefted fruit, it can be surmised that this fruit also served as a symbol for the Yoni.

Seeds associated with the Yoni include the cardamom plant and the coco-de-mer. The cardamom seed is used as a meditation symbol in intimate Tantric rituals. After other preparations, including touching one another's bodies, the practitioners each open a cardamom seed and meditate on its shape, which resembles that of the Yoni.

An unambiguous example of naturally occurring Yoni symbology is the coco-de-mer (see figure 34), the seed of a special type of palm[**] that grows in no other place in the world but on two of the Seychelles Islands.[***] The seed is a huge double coconut, the shape of which resembles a woman's parted thighs with the vulva clearly visible. When found on the Indian shoreline the seed was considered a miraculous coconut from the sea; the coco-de-mer thus earned a status comparable to that of the meteorites venerated elsewhere. Being apparently born from the female element water and given by the sea to the people, the coco-de-mer was a valuable and sought-after symbol of the Great Goddess. This combined with its obvious vulva shape contributed to the coco-de-mer becoming one of India's most revered symbols of the Yoni.

One also finds the universal shape of the Yoni present within the world's fauna, especially among certain creatures of the ocean, such as mollusks and shells. For instance, the conch shell is regarded not only as a representation of the Yoni but as a foremost symbol of the feminine in general. In Tibet and India, where conch shells are often used as musical instruments, the sound that emerges from the shell's spirals is considered to be a symbol of eternity and of pure, primordial space, a concept that equals the element of ether in western Hermeticism.

Less ethereal is the symbology of the cowrie shell, one of the earliest forms of currency traded in Africa and Asia;[****] in fact, the Latin name for one variety of cowrie is *Cypraea moneta*. The value attached to such shells, however, comes from a more spiritual basis. In a great many cultures the beautiful cowrie (see page 28, figure 37) was considered a symbol of the Divine Yoni, and for that reason was used as a fertility charm. The cowrie was also believed to have healing and regenerative powers. Whether it was worn in necklaces or placed in graves to accompany the dead on their journey into a new cycle, the cowrie provided the devotee with an especially intimate connection to the Great Mother. Cowrie shells were considered sacred in such diverse societies as those of the

[*] Although regarded as slang by dictionary definition, in contemporary German the word meaning "plum" (German: *Pflaume*) is a common expression for the female genitals. Similar associations are found in Dutch and other languages.
[**] *Lodicea sechellarium*
[***] The islands are Curieuse and Praslin.
[****] Cowrie shells were used as currency into the twentieth century among tribes of Papua New Guinea and some of the Melanesian Islands.

FIGURE 34
A nineteenth-century coco-de-mer, a rare type of coconut that grows on the Seychelles Islands.

FIGURE 35
The similarity to the vulva of this Caribbean Venus shell, nicknamed Venus's Garter in Europe, was reported in great detail by 18th-century botanist and taxonomist Carolus Linnaeus.

Polynesian Islands, Africa, India, and the Mediterranean, as well as in the Europe of 20,000 B.C.E.

The scallop, another marine mollusk, is an ancient European symbol of the Yoni, used as such from the far northern shores of the Norsemen to the southeastern borders of Greek civilization. The English *scallop*, with etymological roots in the Norse *skalpr* ("sheath, vagina"), has similar connotations to *kteis*, the Greek name for the mollusk. *K teis* is not only used to refer to this specific shell (see page 19) and sometimes to the cowrie as well; it is also a term widely used for the outer and visible female genitals, an equivalent to the Latin *vulva*. When Sandro Botticelli (1445–1510) painted the famous *Birth of Venus*, he consciously used the kteis/scallop to represent the Yoni of the sea out of which this goddess of love and sexuality was born.

The most Yoni-like of all shells is the oyster. Although little is known about the oyster being imbued with mythical or spiritual powers, it does have a reputation as a potent aphrodisiac, most likely based on a shape and texture that so clearly resembles the yoni of certain women.

Given the preceding discussion, we might detect a preoccupation among many ancient cultures with the shape of the Yoni. In our contemporary society, such deep interest is often explained away as the expressions of those who are either sexually frustrated or sexually addicted. However, although the sexual aspect of the yoni can never be forgotten, this was—and is—not the major focus in Yoni worship. The Yoni and everything of its shape was considered a sacred and archetypal symbol of the Divine. As such, it was likely approached with great feeling and thought, similar to the way in which a Buddhist approaches a statue of the great teacher, a practicing Christian approaches the altar and cross, or a conservative Jew approaches the sacred scrolls of the Torah.

To ancient cultures the Yoni symbolized the Goddess, and the Goddess was everywhere. As we will see in the next chapter, later generations of more cerebral and intellectually minded people invented new symbols based on the old ones, sometimes staying close to the original but oftentimes—perhaps out of a growing estrangement from the physical body and a sexuality free of shame—making those symbols more abstract and less intimate.

Figure 36
In anthropology, the association between appearance and reputation is known as sympathetic magic. Oysters thus have the reputation of an aphrodisiac because they look so much like a Yoni after they are poached.

Figure 37
Cowrie shells like this one (Cypraea annulus) *from the Maldives Islands were valued as currency and fertility charms throughout Africa and Oceania.*

▼

THE SACRED TRIANGLE, THE HOLY GRAIL, AND OTHER SYMBOLS

Concentrate on the triangle of origination in the midst of space.

HEVAJRA TANTRA

It is not only in nature that one finds the Yoni abundantly symbolized. Symbols of the Yoni occur often within the context of sacred art and architecture, sometimes in quite surprising places. This is not only true for the more or less veiled illustrations and allusions of alchemists, Qabbalists, Rosicrucians, and others. It is equally true even within the context of Christianity, a religion that neither respects the power of women nor encourages any form of sexuality. (See chapter 5 for depictions of the Yoni on the walls of Christian churches and monasteries.)

Of the many geometric symbols that represent the Yoni, probably the best known are the

downward-pointing triangle and the vesica piscis, or mandorla. Many religious paintings and esoteric diagrams incorporate at least one of these symbols to transmit a message of homage to the Yoni.

The downward-pointing triangle is one of the most abstract and commonly used symbols to represent the Yoni; quite often its meaning goes unrecognized except by those who have a certain degree of esoteric knowledge. For example, in alchemy and astrology this triangle is used to represent the elements of water and earth, the feminine principle, the natural world—all those concepts that are essentially female. The Greek mathematician and initiate Pythagoras

(580–495 B.C.E.) considered the triangle sacred not only because of its perfect shape, but also because it was a symbol of universal fertility. A well-known symbol, Solomon's seal, uses two intersecting triangles to represent the merging of male/solar and female/lunar energies, making this a Western version of the Chinese yin/yang symbol (see glossary). This symbol of the intersecting triangles, commonly known in Hebrew as the Star of David, was also important in the cultures of ancient Greece, India, and the Yucatán.

In the East the triangle has a long history of associations with the Yoni and female energy, as can be seen in yantras and mandalas dedicated to various goddesses and in the many triangles composing the Sri Yantra. In Tantric Buddhism, the triangle is interpreted as the "source of the dharma"▾ (T: Chos 'byung) and as the "gate of all that is born." In the words of the venerable Chögyam Trungpa, the triangle is the "cosmic cervix." The Hevajra Tantra aptly says: "Concentrate on the triangle of origination in the midst of space."

The triangle also appears in the yoni and mahayoni mudras, two of the many specific and canonized postures of the hands and fingers practiced in mainstream Buddhism and Hinduism and in Tantric ritual. The yoni mudra is also an asana or full-body posture in which the forward-bent torso, together with folded legs and arms, creates a downward-pointing triangle.

Another widespread symbol of the Yoni is the mandorla. An almond-shaped design

FIGURE 39 (TOP)
A contemporary painting on the walls of a former palace in Vrindavan, India.

FIGURE 40
Tripur Bhairavi, dedicated to the goddess Bhairavi, is another traditional yantra that makes use of the triangle.

THE YONI

▾ The Sanskrit word *dharma* translates as "teaching" or "religion."

FIGURE 41
In this fifteenth-century painting,
the artist has embedded Mary
and her divine child within a
mandorla, a universal symbol of
the Goddess and the Yoni.

known in sacred geometry as the vesica piscis,▾ this symbol is often used to represent such concepts as divinity and sacredness—quite fitting for the Yoni, the gateway of life. The mandorla appears quite often in Christian iconography, where it is said to symbolize the flame of the spirit. Considering that the Christian Church freely appropriated symbols from its predecessors for its own use, it is not unlikely that the mandorla-shaped aureole or halo that is often seen surrounding Mary, the Virgin Queen of Heaven, is in fact an indication of the powers of the ancient Goddess.

A symbol not unlike the mandorla is the lozenge. However, rather than having the roundness of the mandorla, the lozenge consists of four straight lines that are more easily engraved into stone, once quite important for people whose writing and drawing had to be done in stone or clay. Although it is a simple geometric form, the lozenge represented the life-giving womb of the Goddess in many cultures, especially those surrounding the Mediterranean Sea.

▾ Geometrically, the vesica piscis consists of two intersecting circles and is related to the golden mean, the measure of perfection on which many works of sacred art are based.

FIGURE 42
A beautiful example
of an argha, a yoni-
shaped vessel used for
offerings and libations
during rituals (see
chapter 4). This argha
is from nineteenth-
century Rajasthan,
India.

Similar in shape to the mandorla is the *argha*, the Yoni-shaped ritual chalice. The argha (S: "bowl") is used to pour libations over the Yoni of either a Goddess statue or a woman who is the central participant in a Yoni Puja ceremony (see chapter 4).

Perhaps the most famous of all chalices is the legendary Holy Grail, a sacred lost relic of Christianity. It is interesting to examine the story of the Holy Grail in light of what we know about pre-Christian Europe. In the Old Religion[▾] of northern Europe, the grail was a sacred chalice thought to contain the life energy of the Great Goddess. Although it was specifically the Celtic/Welsh goddess Cerridwen who was in charge of the sacred relic, the grail and its powers were not solely hers. Cerridwen, a deity associated with nature,

[▾] *Old Religion* is a term used by Wiccans (modern witches) to describe the religion that focused on pre-Christian goddesses and gods.

water, blood, and the life force, was regarded as one of three goddesses who together constituted an ancient lunar trinity collectively known as Druan Gwen. The Triple Goddess/trinity image is one that occurs worldwide and corresponds to the three visible phases of the moon and to the three major phases in the life of women: prepubescent girl, menstruating woman, and postmenopausal wise crone. Cerridwen, guardian of the grail, represents the last of these phases, with the younger goddesses Arianrhod and Blodeuwedd representing phases one and two respectively.[▼]

During the time of the Crusades, the conquering potentates tended to incorporate the mythology and symbology of important native goddesses by transforming them into saints or by adapting their festivals and transforming them with Christian symbols and content. Thus was the grail of the Goddess incorporated into Christian mythology in the twelfth century, at which time it became both a symbol and an object considered to have held the blood of Christ. This is the Holy Grail from which the privileged drank the wine of the sacrament, the sacred relic interwoven with the legends of Avalon and King Arthur, Morgaine and Lancelot, Parsifal and the Knights of the Round Table.[▼▼] Given all this, it is interesting to look at figure 43, which shows the landscape around Glastonbury, the mythical place where the Holy Grail is supposed to have been hidden. The hill and pathways of Glastonbury bear a striking resemblance to the shape of the Yoni.

Many adepts and would-be adepts of the hermetic tradition in Europe and the United States also use a sacred cup, a Holy Grail, to hold the wine of the sacrament. Within such circles, however, the wine is not the sour red wine symbolic of the blood of Christ. Considering that the expression "wine of the sacrament" can also refer to the mingled male and female secretions of the participants in certain rituals,[1] this wine may be a much sweeter nectar.

It was not so much the Yoni but the uterus that inspired alchemists. The Latin word *alembic* (from the Arabic *al-anbiq*) describes an alchemical instrument used to distill certain chemical/magical fluids. However, within the secret language often used by alchemists, the term was also used as a code word for the uterus, a place where equally magical fluids are produced.

The variety of objects and symbols people over the ages have invented and used in order to express the adoration they felt for the Goddess is truly remarkable. Figure 44 shows a votive tablet from Greece depicting the Yoni of the ancient goddess Daphoene (later Daphne) and bearing the inscription *Daphne Dedicates This to Zeus*. Daphne, who was eventually demoted to the status of tree nymph, is unlikely to have actually made such a dedication, since Zeus is a deity known for simply taking whatever he wanted by force, including sex. The inscription is another example of the ways in which adherents

FIGURE 43
The shape of the pathways leading up and around Glastonbury Hill clearly indicates the Grail's association with the Old Religion.

FIGURE 44
A marble votive tablet from Athens, allegedly the Yoni of the goddess Daphne.

[▼] Most literature distinguishes only one dimension of the first two phases, disregarding the many manifestations of prepubescent and fertile energy. The phase-one woman is simply called virgin, an ambiguous term and not to the point. The phase-two woman is called mother, an incorrect description considering that not all women want to be mothers and some may never even want to unite with a man.

[▼▼] Marion Zimmer Bradley's novel *The Mists of Avalon* comes closest to conveying what is most likely the true story of the Holy Grail.

FIGURE 45 (TOP)
This hollow silver box from twentieth-century Ethiopia is used as a pendant and an amulet.

FIGURE 46 (ABOVE)
A carved ivory amulet from the Kongolo area of eastern Zaire.

FIGURE 47 (LEFT)
This amulet of carved bone is worn by the Bashi people of Kivu, eastern Zaire.

FIGURE 48 (RIGHT)
A carved piece of wood that is used as a stamp in India.

THE YONI

34

of the Sky God religion of classical, Olympic Greece twisted indigenous myths and made earlier deities into servants of their own (later) gods.

In some places the Yoni in symbolic form becomes an altar itself. This is common in India, where large, beautiful shells resembling the Yoni inside and out are embedded into a block of wood that is painted with a triangle. This altar, hidden to visitors by a veil, serves as the private house shrine.

As well as employing such symbols in celebration and ritual, Yoni symbology was incorporated into the activities of everyday life. For example, all over the world people have used Yoni-shaped amulets for protection and Yoni-shaped charms for fertility. The fact that we have few examples of such personal works of Yoni art is largely due to the perishability of the materials used in producing such objects. Though contemporary tribal peoples have been subjected to intense missionary activity, the continuing existence of such pieces among them shows the persistence of the beliefs that have shaped humanity since the beginning of time. Contemporary examples of such amulets from twentieth-century Ethiopia, Zaire, and the Netherlands are shown in figures 45–47 and in figure 75 on page 71. The ubiquitous horseshoe, widely regarded as a symbol of good luck, derives its amulet-like function from the fact that it was, in centuries past, another symbol of the Yoni.

In whatever direction of the compass and in whatever time, the Yoni is seen everywhere: painted on rock walls, cut into river stone, fashioned from marble or earth. Considering that our ancestors often kept to rivers when traveling, both for guidance and for the Goddess-given supply of fresh water, it is easy to imagine how artisan and weaponmaker alike would be fascinated by a beautiful piece of stone, rounded and

smoothed by the waters, and turn it into a symbol of her. It seems that gifted and inspired travelers, grateful perhaps to their Goddess for guidance and nourishment along the way, took to marking such a stone with the most simple but clearly recognizable sign of the Yoni. A small incision, a laborious task given neolithic tools, turned an objet trouvé into a sign of thanksgiving and a token that the anonymous traveler had honored her. Other artisans would laboriously turn a piece of marble into the lower torso of a goddess or pick up a suitably shaped piece of stone and turn it into a representation of the Divine Yoni.

Generations later, with new and more sophisticated techniques available, worshipers of the Goddess and the Yoni no longer needed to create single pieces of art but would simply replicate her sacred symbol wherever desired and suitable with the help of wooden stamps.

Whatever the medium, the message is always the same: Humanity at large, thousands of years following the first paintings and rock carvings in the paleolithic caves of southern Europe, still worships the Goddess and her Yoni. In the next chapter we will look at some contemporary rituals that have at their heart Yoni-worship ceremonies of old.

▼

4

SECRET RITUALS AND TEMPLES TO HER

The practitioner who utters the words Yoni Yoni
at the time of his prayers,
for him the Yoni shall be favorable,
granting enjoyment and liberation.

YONI TANTRA, PATALA III[1]

In a world pillaged and overrun by male-dominated hordes attempting to rid humanity of all vestiges of women's power, the practice of Goddess worship was driven underground, and rituals celebrating the Goddess had to be elegantly covered in order to survive. Spectacular sacred ceremonies once shared by all in the community were forced to retreat behind several veils of secrecy. What was once general knowledge was of necessity hidden in the form of esoteric codes and symbolism, able to be penetrated only by those entrusted with the key.

rituals taking place in the inner rather than the outer world. In contemporary India, for example, the Goddess and her Yoni are still venerated in many ways; yet, worship of the live Yoni is a strongly guarded secret that is hardly mentioned in the otherwise extensive and detailed literature describing the various religious schools of the vast Indian subcontinent. In the same way, most rituals that were once practiced in material reality within the esoteric teachings of Tibetan Buddhism are now internalized: instead of actually drinking the nectar from the Goddess's Yoni, one simply visualizes the transfer of her sexual energy to one's own body.

In the attempt to save Goddess worship from complete annihilation, real-life events and ceremonies were turned into exercises of the imagination,

When we study the Tantric practice of Yoni

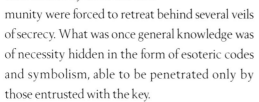

Puja (the Holy Mass of the Vulva) or the Shingon fire ritual, or when we look at Assam's Yonimandala, the cave where Mother Earth menstruates once every year, we are peering directly into the deep past of humanity. This experience of seeing the veiled or muted practices of Yoni worship is similar to looking at the stars and knowing that the eyes actually receive light that was emitted thousands of years ago. For example, we discover that priests of the Shingon school in twentieth-century Japan still honor the Goddess of old when they perform a fire ritual, an ancient ceremony originating at the dawn of humanity. On the outside, there is no evidence suggesting the presence of anyone or anything female in the proceedings. On an unseen level, though, as the Shingon initiate learns, the fire is actually kindled between the open legs of a nude, albeit nonphysical, woman. Another surprising example is the strong suggestion of Yoni worship at the very heart of the world's most patriarchal religion. Although the story says that Muhammad, the prophet of Islam, had all idols destroyed when taking over the sacred city of Mecca, he apparently did not dare to touch the great Black Stone from heaven; he simply restyled the Yoni of the goddess Al'Lat into the hand of Allah.

Later in the chapter we will examine the evidence of Goddess worship at the root of Shingon and Islamic practices. First let us look at some of the many forms of Yoni worship found on the Indian subcontinent today.

YONI PUJA IN CONTEMPORARY INDIA

The Sanskrit word *puja* is usually translated as "worship." Linguistically there is nothing wrong with that translation; however, for a native speaker the word *puja* carries emotional connotations of the same magnitude that Holy Mass carries for Christians. *Worship* sounds rather detached—a word that belongs to the terminology of anthropologists rather than to the vocabulary of someone actively practicing her or his faith. With this in mind, we can approach the subject of Yoni Puja understanding the depth of feeling that underlies its practice.

In abstract terms, a Yoni Puja can be defined as a sacred ritual during which the Yoni is worshiped. While a sculpture, a painting, or a sanctified natural object may be used as the focus of veneration, Yoni Puja can also be performed by worshiping the Yoni in her living form. During the ceremony, the worshipper engages in one-pointed meditation on the chosen representation of the Goddess. In the religious practice that is still very much alive in present-day India, a Yoni Puja—a ritual that dates back thousands of years—is a complex, detailed, intimate (to some), and strange (to others) manner of religious worship.

In practical detail, this ritual can take many forms. Considering the vastness of the Indian subcontinent and the multisectarian nature of the religion known as Hinduism, the fact that there are a multitude of variations of Yoni Puja is quite understandable and should come as no surprise. However, several ritual elements and distinct symbologies constitute a kind of blueprint for the Yoni Puja, regardless of variations in form. There are several subdivisions of the Yoni Puja, the basic subdivision being the inner and outer

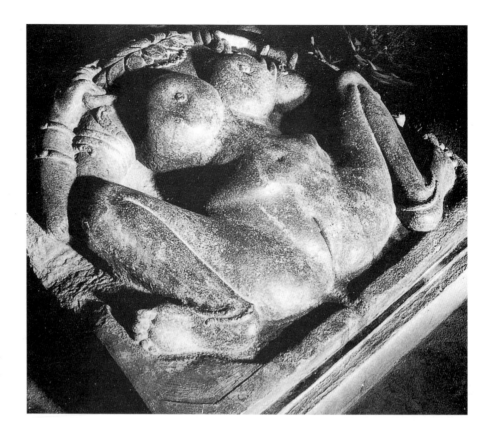

FIGURE 50
A unique altar of the goddess,
clearly designed for the practice
of Yoni Puja. This eighth-
century stone sculpture clearly
shows the rim where the
libations poured upon the Yoni
would collect.

pujas,[†] each of which can occur in either an ordinary form or a secret form. The secret form is again subdivided into the three categories of adoration, magic, and meditation, the latter being the most covert form of worship.

In ordinary Yoni Puja, performed with a sculpture of the Devi (S: "goddess") or with a woman (S: *stri*) as her living representative, five liquids representing the five elements of Indian cosmology are poured consecutively over the Yoni and are collected in a vessel below the thighs. The element earth is represented by yogurt, the element water by actual water, fire by honey, air by milk, and ether by a type of edible oil.[††] The final mixture of the five libations, empowered by such direct and intimate contact with the living Goddess, is then consumed by those present at the ritual. Such libations are often simply interpreted by outsiders as an offering to the Divine; however, once these substances have been offered to the Goddess, she, having purified and energized them, returns the offering as a gift (S: *prasad*) to her worshipers.

Such elemental symbolism permeates most forms of worship in India. In other pujas different substances are used; yet, they carry the same underlying symbolism. Any traveler

---

[†] In this context, the term *inner puja* refers to a practice carried out through visualization rather than one that is happening visibly in the material world. The term *outer puja* refers to a ritual of one or more persons venerating the Yoni either in the symbolic form of an object or in the live form of a woman as representative of the Goddess. The latter type of Yoni Puja is often performed in mixed groups, although sometimes the ceremony is restricted to one gender or the other.

[††] To any reader who may feel inspired to enact such a ritual in private, I recommend using a high-quality and good-tasting oil. Sesame oil and walnut oil are both well suited to this ritual.

to India will have seen pujas performed in which fire and water are used with burning incense (the sense of smell being related to earth), a peacock feather (related to air), and a conch shell (the sense of sound being related to ether) that is blown continuously amidst the sounds of bells and cymbals. Those attending a puja will usually offer five different fruits or other substances, such as milk, flower petals, or rice, to the deity. In this regard we can see that the Yoni Puja follows mainstream Hindu ceremonial form, however special and secret the ritual may otherwise be.

In the case of a Yoni Puja practiced with an object such as the altar of the Devi shown in figure 50 or with a natural object such as a coco-de-mer (see figure 34 on page 27), the strength of the energies imparted to the prasad (S: "divine gift") is dependent upon how well and by whom the object has been consecrated and sanctified. In a Yoni Puja performed with a living woman (S: *stri puja*), the merits of the practice—the strength of the transference of power from the Yoni via the liquid substances to the participants—is dependent upon the woman who serves as the focus of worship. Of all stri pujas, the most simple is the worship of a young girl of sixteen years (S: *kumari puja*). Although the number 16 is regarded in India as the number of perfection, and although she will first be consecrated by a priest, the girl's "perfection"—her nubility and beauty—does not lend her any of the powers that are possessed by a woman of higher degree. In the latter case, the woman at the center of worship is a *yogini*, a title reserved for someone who has been initiated into the precepts and techniques of Tantra and who, as such, is also more mature.[▼] Again, the powers transferred from her Yoni are comparatively weak when compared with those of a woman who is the channel of power in an even higher type of practice. Here, at the summit of all Yoni Pujas, the woman representing the Goddess is a full-fledged guru;[▼▼] the powers transferred from her Yoni are strongest and most suited to raising the consciousness of those who imbibe the mixture of liquids that have been purified and empowered by contact with her naked Yoni, her flame of intelligence.

As mentioned previously, the secret outer pujas can be divided into three categories: rituals of adoration, rituals of magic, and meditation rituals. Among these, the first two are easiest to describe. Before the visible Yoni, either of a living woman or of an image of the Goddess, the worshipers offer their general prayers (adoration) or chant mantras while beseeching her to grant them wishes of all kinds (magic), wishes that range from the personal ("Please cure my mother" or "Please give me a son") to the egocentric ("Let me have success in business and make me rich"). Nothing in these rituals could possibly be classified as "sexual" or "obscene"; the participants simply ask for a little attention from the Divine for their personal ambitions, problems, and sufferings. These kinds of prayers are

---

[▼] In general use, the Sanskrit term yogini refers to a female practitioner of yoga, with yogi or yogin as the male variant. Yogini is also the generic term for a pantheon of between eight and sixty-four goddesses, usually regarded as manifestations of the Great Goddess Durga. Relative to the context of Yoni Puja, the Hatha Yoga Pradipika (III.99 as translated by Feuerstein) defines a yogini as a female initiate who can "preserve her own genital ejaculate" and who is able to suck semen into herself with the help of special techniques, eventually directing it to her brain. Having thus mixed with her yin essence, the transformed substance is thought to greatly strengthen the practitioner.

[▼▼] Kumari puja and puja with a yogini are easier to arrange; fully initiated female gurus are quite difficult to find.

The divine Yoni is brilliant as tens of millions of suns, and cool as tens of millions of moons.

Above the Yoni, there is a small and subtle flame, whose form is intelligence.

SHIVA SAMHITA,
17TH CENTURY, INDIA

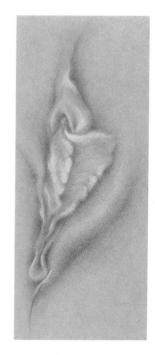

FIGURE 51
Flower of Passion *by Christina Camphausen.*

Secret Rituals

offered and encouraged in most religions, the major difference between them being that some direct their prayers to an invisible but jealous father figure in heaven; some to a naked, crucified man; some to his weeping mother; and some to the source and seat of life, the gateway that connects the inner womb of gestation with the outer reality of human existence.

The Rahasya Puja, the most secret of all Yoni Pujas, is a ceremony consisting of the meditation aspect of both secret and overt worship. In a Rahasya Puja, the practitioner is alone with the woman who has agreed to serve as the focus of devic energies. This woman may be his wife▾ or lover, an initiate, or perhaps a *veshya*, a professional woman specializing in such services. The worshiper sits between the woman's open legs and, with complete concentration and unwavering awareness, goes through a cycle of ritual actions, each of which represents one of the five elements.

With the element ether in mind, the practitioner moves his hands across the woman's body, from her legs to her breasts, in large circles. This movement is repeated for five to ten minutes or until attention is fully focused on ether as one constituent element through which the Goddess makes manifest all things. Next, with the element air in mind, the practitioner restricts the movement of his hands to her belly and thighs, once again repeating the strokes until one-pointed attention on the air element is achieved. During the third stage, with the attention now focused on the Yoni as representing the fire element, the genital area is stroked in a repetitive upward movement. In the next stage the stroking is changed to a downward direction, symbolizing the element water. Finally, the element earth is given expression by pressing one hand, softly but firmly, against the woman's Yoni, resting there until the ritual finds its natural end. The entire ritual can take an hour or longer to complete.

The practice of Yoni Puja varies regionally and among different schools in regard to the succession of steps and actions taken; the basic structure of the ceremony and its focus, however, remain constant. Thus, a practitioner may start with the ritual celebrating the earth element rather than ether, or enact fire before water. Such differences in practice are of no consequence—what matters are the dedication and single-minded attention of the practitioner, combined with the power inherent in the object of veneration. It is this combination that enables the raising of one's awareness and influences the potential for liberation inherent in these rituals. The fundamental prerequisite is the ability of the practitioner to perform this ritual with a deep love and respect for the powers of woman, for the seat of life, for the Goddess.▾▾

Other Tantric sects, embracing and utilizing all manifestations of life in order to find enlightenment, often go much further. (Researchers and scholars of the early twentieth

---

▾ Different scriptures and teachings vary considerably on this topic. Some say that worship with the married partner or other family members is strictly taboo; others explicitly encourage such practice.

▾▾ The practice described here is not that of an obscure group of practitioners but is rather a standard practice of mainstream Tantric Hinduism. The information disclosed above, passed on to me by someone who participated in such rituals only a decade ago, proves that worship of the Goddess and the Yoni has survived in India up to the present day.

century often found these practices too shocking to report on honestly.) The Yoni Puja is practiced among these sects, though in some Tantric texts we find mention of this ritual under alternative names such as *bhagayagya*. Besides the obvious fact that a unique and special one-pointedness can be achieved by contemplative concentration on the Yoni, it becomes clear from sacred texts such as the Yoni Tantra▾ that the major aim of a Tantric Yoni Puja is the ritual creation of a subtle energy and/or liquid called *yonitattva*, or, in special cases, *yonipuspa*.

Whereas in other Yoni Puja ceremonies the initiated woman (the yogini) is specifically trained to not become sexually aroused by the attention to her body, and especially to her Yoni, in more esoteric Tantric practices the sexual energies are awakened on purpose. In these rituals the Yoni is not only adored and worshiped, it is also stimulated and excited and sometimes even penetrated, depending on which holy scripture the sect follows. No mixture of yogurt, honey, and oil is consumed by these worshipers. The most esoteric of Tantrics in their most secret modes of worship consume the juices of love produced by the woman/Goddess or produced by mingling the female juices with those of the male. Two-thirds of this yonitattva, or divine nectar, is mixed with wine and drunk by the congregation; the remaining one-third is offered to the Goddess.

This type of Yoni Puja is sometimes celebrated with a menstruating woman, producing the even more powerful liquid known as yonipuspa (S: "flower of the Yoni"). Although this practice is forbidden by most texts and within many sects, it is specifically advocated in the Yoni Tantra.▾▾ So great is the supposed merit of this ritual that the practitioners who make the Yoni Puja their sole mode of worship are excused from any other ritual obligation.

It may be difficult today for readers steeped in a Judeo-Christian morality—one that has created an aura of shame and disgust about the body, the genitals, and most everything that has to do with sexuality—to imagine how such practices came into existence. Such readers probably ask: "How, in the name of all that is holy, can anyone connect such practices with religion? How can anyone even dare to claim that there is anything sacred about touching and kissing that part of the body?" To those who would voice objections along this line, a worshiper of the Goddess and of the Yoni might answer in the same tone of disbelief: "How, in the name of all that is holy, can anyone think that the place where all of us come from, the very place of our birth, is a place of shame? It is the most important, the most powerful, the most beautiful place on earth. Worship it with all your heart, or you will be lost!"

THE YONIMANDALA OF ASSAM

One of India's most popular myths tells the story of how the goddess Sati was dismembered, her body falling down to earth limb for limb and piece for piece. Sati is venerated

---

▾ The Yoni Tantra is a sacred text from eastern Bengal, the region known today as Bangladesh. The text is dated to the eleventh century, but may be slightly older. In the bibliography, see Schoterman.

▾▾ Such practices concerning menstruation have been found not only in India but elsewhere in the world. Certain groups among the early Christian Gnostics, a group considered heretical by the church, also made ritual use of the menstrual fluid.

throughout India under many names, including Shakti, Durga, and Kali. The story of Sati's dismemberment goes like this.

Once the goddess Sati felt so deeply insulted by the fact that she and her husband Shiva had not been invited to an important sacrificial feast that, in a fit of rage and protest, she killed herself. Almost mad with anger and grief, the god Shiva wandered the world restlessly, carrying with him the corpse of his beloved. Not only did Shiva neglect all his duties; in his anguish and fury he destroyed all he encountered.

In order to end this madness and to bring Shiva back to his senses, the god Vishnu followed Shiva in his wanderings, finally cutting Sati's body to pieces with his sword until nothing remained of her. The bits and pieces of her body fell down to earth, each landing in a different place, mainly in northern India and the neighboring country of Nepal.

Shrines and temples, which collectively came to be known as *shaktipiths* (S: "shrine of the Goddess," "seat of power"), were subsequently built in those places. Sati's Yoni is said to have fallen at the Manobhavaguha Cave at Mount Nila, a cave that harbors a Yoni-shaped cleft. The cave is regarded as the *axis mundi*, the center of the universe. The shrine at this cave is known as the Kamakhya Pitha; the stone with its cleft is called the Yonimandala.

The Kamakhya Pitha is a famous sacred site. Located near Gauhati, a city of the ancient kingdom of Kamarupa (present-day Assam), it comprises a cave sanctuary and a shrine. The present-day foundations of the temple date from the sixteenth century, but the cave itself has been a sacred place for much longer. Most venerated among the fifty-one pithas,[*] this cave sanctuary is visited by pilgrims who come to worship the Goddess's Yoni and to drink from the red waters it produces. The celebrated shrine is named after the goddess Kamakhya or Kamaksa, who is thought to reside here. In Tantric literature, Kamakhya is regarded as the aspect of the Great Goddess prepared for sexual play and enjoyment.

Through the shrine one can, if allowed, access the actual cave sanctuary that houses the Yonimandala. The cleft is moist throughout the year because of a natural spring within the cave. Here one can also witness the menstruation of the Goddess, an event that is celebrated during Sravanah, the period between mid-July and mid-August. Where the sacred stone takes the shape of her Yoni, a red and intoxicating water wells out of the its cleft.[**] This seasonal event is celebrated with great enthusiasm by Indian worshipers.

In the absence of photographic evidence (Assam is difficult to get into for political reasons, and the cave is even more closely guarded), we must rely on sparse information gleaned from sacred texts and on the reports of a few persevering non-Hindu travelers who have gained admittance to the temple.[***] The Yogini Tantra, a sacred text of approximately

[*] The number of holy places with pitha status varies according to the texts of the different traditions connected with them.

[**] Brought on by the first activities of the monsoon season, the water contains high levels of iron oxide and traces of arsenic.

[***] Two recent (1995) visitors who gained entrance into the shrine of Gauhati and its famous Kamakhya Pitha through persistence and fortuitous circumstance told me the story of their travels. The visitors were permitted to stay at Gauhati for one day only and, although they were allowed by priests to visit the sanctuary, they were absolutely forbidden to take a camera inside. While being guided through the labyrinthine pathways that lead to the Yonimandala, they were required to practice all the prescribed ritual movements and offerings before they reached the well that brings forth the sacred waters.

FIGURE 52
Every day, people visit the temple
at Gauhati in Assam in order to
pray to the goddess Kamakhya.
The inner sanctum of the temple
contains the well that is regarded as
the goddess's menstruating yoni.

the eleventh century, tells that the well within the cave "reaches down into the netherworld" and that the actual opening of the Yoni "measures twelve fingers all around."[2] According to local belief and attesting once more to the miraculous powers associated with
the Goddess's Yoni, it is said that those who drink from the well will not be reborn; that is,
they will no longer be bound to earthly life but will be liberated in the highest sense of the
word, the ultimate aim within a religion that regards the human condition as eternal bond-
age to lives full of suffering.

As seat of the Goddess's Yoni, the Kamakhya Pitha has a competitor in the Nepali
temple of the goddess Guheshvari. Something of a hybrid goddess, Guheshvari is worshiped by both the Hindu and Buddhist populations of Nepal. Her worshipers believe
Guheshvari to be the divine presence of the *guhe* (N: "yoni") of the goddess Sati. They believe this beautiful temple outside Kathmandu also contains the Divine Yoni and give it
the status of a sacred pitha. The temple is only one kilometer away from Pashupatinath,

Nepal's famous temple dedicated to Shiva. Guheshvari's pitha features a golden oval platform shaped in the form of a Yoni, with an "unfathomable opening"[3] at its center that is kept covered by a ceremonial water vessel.

BUDDHIST VISUALIZATIONS

While Tantric practices are considered by many to be pleasure seeking in the name of religion, what is popularly known about Buddhist teachings creates an image of virtuousness and austerity. It may therefore come as a surprise to many readers that Tibetan Buddhism, as well as some schools of Japanese Buddhism, not only makes use of sexual imagery but also calls attention to the Yoni and especially to the energies contained in the liquids that flow from this source of sources.

FIGURE 53
A human yogini of the eighth century, Mahasukhasiddhi ("Adept of Great Bliss"), was one of those Tibetan women who initiated male practitioners into the Tantric arts. Her Tibetan name is Naljorma Dewa Ngodrub Chenpo.

The writings of the second Dalai Lama, Gendun Gyatso (1475–1542), leave no doubt that the early adepts of certain schools▾ used much sexual imagery in their visualizations and also found value in the outer enactment of such inner visions. Most lamas of our day prefer to keep quiet about this topic; some even deny that these techniques—proven and tested by generations of lamas and adepts, shamans and shamanesses, yogis and yoginis—have ever been a part of their great lineage. However, I invite you to make your own conclusions after reading the following examples from Gendun Gyatso's *Transmission of the Wisdom Dakini*.

This particular visualization, written as instruction for men, first recommends the practitioner visualize himself as the deity Heruka. Once this deity is fully embodied, a triangle of white light will appear at the level of the practitioner's eyebrows. This downward pointing triangle, a universal symbol of the Goddess and her Yoni, is to be visualized as connecting the adept's two ears, with the third angle pointing to the root of the tongue. The true nature of this triangle is then described as follows: It "appears in the nature of blissful wisdom and gives rise to ecstasy," symbolizing "the wisdom of innate great bliss, or higher tantric consciousness." It "has the shape of the consort's vagina, thus symbolizing innate wisdom, and its three sides represent the three doors of liberation."[4]

▾ In the absence of a detailed genealogy of Vajrayana Buddhism, the schools referred to here are the Kagyud-pa and its subsect, the Karma Kagyu.

In another part of the same text the reader is given a technique for receiving the four "powerful initiations." Visualizing upon one's own head the Goddess Vajraishvaridhatu bound in a sexual embrace with the Buddha Vajradhara, the practitioner then sees how "from the point of their sexual union flows forth the precious nectar," a liquid that the practitioner should then visualize as entering his or her own body.[5]

Similar to the above practice is the exercise known as purification by means of the goddess Nairatmika, the Egoless One. The *Transmission of the Wisdom Dakini* recommends the following:

> In the space before you, visualize the Dakini Nairatmika. She is blue in color and holds a curved knife and skull cup. One recites the mantra OM AH SVAHA, causing blue lights to radiate forth from her body. They enter one's own body via one's sexual organ, and then the Egoless One herself enters one's body via the same passage. She melts into light, and one's body becomes filled with a bluish radiance.... All becomes pristine emptiness.[6]

Such visualizations are not meant solely for male practitioners. An example of a secret visualization technique best suited for female followers of the path comes to us from the Black Hat sect, a branch of the Karma Kagyu.

> Imagine that your body is in the form of the Wisdom-Goddess, a complete virgin-girl, naked, with hair flowing. Imagine yourself as her, in the center of an effulgence of light, holding an elixir bowl close to her heart and garlanded with red flowers. Think to yourself that the Guru enters you through your open yoni and resides in your heart. Then imagine the Wisdom-Goddess above the crown of your head, having just consummated the act of love; she is naked, with disheveled hair, and her yoni is moist and overflowing with sexual secretions. Her three eyes are filled with erotic emotion and look toward the vast expanse of the sky, which, as she begins to dance, becomes filled with similar forms of herself.[7]

In these visualizations the flow of energy is mostly from the deity to the practitioner. However, Tantra is not a one-way road; there also are visualizations meant to help transfer energies from the practitioner to the deity. One of these techniques is called the yoga of consciousness transference. Taught by the Mahasiddha Naropa and the Yogini Niguma, both of the eleventh century, these techniques can be used at any time but especially at the moment of one's death. At a particular moment in time, both during daily meditation and in the process of dying, one's mind, in the form of a white letter A, shoots up the central channel along the spine and then leaves the body via an aperture at the top of the skull. The mind, having left the body, flows toward the Goddess, the Holy Mother Vajra Yogini, and enters into her "via the passage of her sexual organ, which is red in color," finally dissolving when it reaches her heart. The mind thus becomes "one with the wisdom of bliss and void of the Vajra Yogini."[8]

अ

FIGURE 54
In the sacred art of Tibetan Buddhism, each deity is depicted according to a strict traditional canon regulating physical proportions as well as tools and symbols accompanying the figure. Dakinis and Yoginis are often shown in a stance and attire that displays their yoni, as is shown in this blueprint for the goddess Vajra Yogini.

GOMA: THE SHINGON FIRE RITUAL OF MODERN JAPAN

In his well-researched and revealing publication *The Tantric Ritual of Japan,* historian and Shingon initiate Richard Payne shows that an ancient and well-preserved ritual, rooted in a shamanic tradition and thought to be a male preserve, still in modern day honors the Goddess and her Yoni as the root of all things.

The Shingon school of Japanese Buddhism has its origins in a Chinese school known as Mi-tsung, the School of Secrets. The Mi-tsung school came into being in the eighth century, when Indian Tantrics came to China and began to spread and teach their knowledge. These imported teachings, similar to those that gave rise to Tibetan Vajrayana Buddhism, were a mixture of ancient shamanic/magical rituals and the rather new teachings of the Buddha (563–483 B.C.E.). Whereas the Chinese School of Secrets did not succeed in gaining a wide following, its Japanese successor did. Today, Shingon (J: "the true word") is the third largest of all Buddhist schools in Japan.

In his book, Payne elucidates the connections between Tantric teachings and the Shingon school.

It is well recognized that there is a historical continuity between the goma [J: "fire ritual," from the Sanskrit *homa*] of present day Japanese Tantric Buddhism and the fire sacrifices known to predate even the earliest Vedas. Elements of the Vedic rituals have been found to be identical with elements of the goma. The Vedic rituals are themselves known to be based on the fire cult introduced into India by Aryan nomads.[9]

The following discussion bears witness to a surprising bit of evidence showing that the Goddess and her Yoni are at the heart of a ritual most often thought to be thoroughly male.

In Greek myth it was Prometheus, a heroic male demigod, who brought the gift of fire to humanity. In fact, in world religions and myths, most of the deities associated with fire are male. As one of the consistent elements in Eastern and Western cosmological, alchemical, and esoteric thought, fire is usually and quite universally regarded as a male force.

However, while the force of fire is rightly regarded as male, its ultimate source seems to be wholly female. When Payne progressed from student to initiated priest in the traditions preserved in Shingon, he came to learn that in present-day Japan, as in India, the priest charged with performing the ancient fire ritual would visualize himself sitting between the open legs of a nude woman—in other words, the Goddess. Describing a Sanskrit fire ritual, the Brhad Aranyika Upanishad states:

> Her lower part is the (sacrificial) altar, her hairs the (sacrificial) grass, her skin the soma press.▼ The two lips of her Yoni are the fire in the middle.[10]

By quoting seldom-reproduced texts from the Upanishads and the Puranas such as this, the author makes it clear that the Goddess and her Yoni, although invisible to outsiders and bystanders, is the central focus of the Japanese goma proceedings.

In the *Puranic Encyclopedia,* editor Vettam Mani comments on a verse from the Agni Purana that states: "The priest performs the rites, himself seated to the west of the Yoni and his head turned to the east."[11] In his commentary Mani states that the Yoni is that of Shakti, the Great Goddess, and that in this ritual circumstance, "the conception of Shakti is that of a woman lying on her back, head towards the east."[12] The ritual scenario is this: The priest sits with his eyes gazing eastward, in the direction of the rising sun. While he prepares and lights the fire, movements he has learned by rote and that no longer require his full attention, his mind is concentrated on the imaginary Yoni of the visualized woman between whose legs he sits.

Considering the unchanging and highly ritualized▼▼ nature of all ceremonies relating to the preservation and creation of fire, this discussion invites us to conclude that even a force universally recognized as male cannot, in the final analysis, exist without the

▼ Soma is an ecstasy-inducing drink imbibed by Vedic priests during certain ceremonies.
▼▼ In the language of scientists, "highly ritualized" means that the activities of a particular ceremony were passed very much unchanged from generation to generation.

FIGURE 55
In this unique Japanese terra-cotta, the Buddha is seen meditating in front of, and perhaps about, the Golden Gate, a Chinese term for the Yoni. Although it may be surprising to many contemporary Buddhists, this sculpture conveys the same message as a passage from the Candamaharosana Tantra, wherein the Buddha is quoted as having said "Take refuge in the yoni of an esteemed woman."

magical power, creativity, and protection of the divine female. Like all other manifestations and expressions of nature, fire needs the Divine Yoni in order to come to life. From the writings of Payne and others, we once again see that truly ancient concepts regarding the life-giving force of the yoni have survived unbroken into the twentieth century.

THE ISLAMIC HOLY OF HOLIES

In his work The Apology, the Arabian philosopher and alchemist al-Kindi (810–872) let the world of the ninth century know that it was the moon goddess Al'Uzza who was enshrined in the Kaaba, and it was her residence that made this site a sacred place. It may be for this candidness as well as other writings that al-Kindi, once first among the Islamic philosophers, lost all influence on Muslim thinkers only a century after his death. This is of great interest considering that the Kaaba at Mecca is the holy of holies of Islam, a truly monotheistic religion not especially friendly toward women and one that is centered on the male Allah as the Supreme Being, certainly not on a woman or a goddess. However, the moon goddess identified by al-Kindi is now known to be one aspect of the Triple Goddess known as Al'Lat,[*] the Great Goddess of the nomadic peoples of Arabia. In pre-Islamic times, it was she who was originally worshipped at the Kaaba. Here at her sacred place, a great stone in the shape of her Yoni, Al'Lat was served by seven priestesses, and her worshipers—in total nudity—circumambulated the sacred black stone seven times, once for each of the seven ancient planets.[**]

As with all triple goddesses, a religious concept found worldwide, Al'Lat has three manifestations, each one connected to a phase of the moon and simultaneously to a phase in a woman's life. The waxing, crescent moon is represented by the maiden Q're or Qure, the young girl and virgin (the Greek Kore); Al'Uzza (A: "the strong one") is the full moon or mother aspect (the mature woman corresponding to the Greek Demeter); and Al'Menat is the waning moon or the crone, a wise old woman concerned with fate and skilled in prophecy and divination.

The Goddess's sacred place, with its life-giving well next to it, attracted pilgrims and worshipers from all over the Arabic peninsula and its neighboring regions. Here, with the sacred black stone as a symbol of her Yoni and in an oasis of life-giving waters, the Goddess resided in her aspect of Earth Mother, creatrix of life and helper of women in childbirth. To this image and focus of energies people came to pray, to ask for offspring and protection, and to celebrate life. It was to this place that the great patriarch Abraham (c. 1900 B.C.E.) came with his wife, Sarah, who was barren for many years. He knowingly chose this place of the Goddess and her fertile powers as the place where he would lie with Hagar, the young and beautiful Egyptian slave who was to bear his first son. For millennia the Kaaba was a place of power where men and women worshiped the Goddess in the form of her Yoni.

In the sixth century the male revolution in the form of Judaism and Christianity that was sweeping through the Near East and Europe reached the tribal peoples of the Arabian deserts. With this revolution came Muhammad, a native-born prophet and the founder of Islam. Muhammad was born c. 570 as a member of the Quraysh, a tribe dedicated to the goddess Qure and the official guardians of the Kaaba. Having lost his parents in early childhood, Muhammad grew up under the guidance of his uncle and his fellow camel herders. Muhammad somehow caught the attention of a rich woman who eventually employed him; after he proved himself successful, she proceeded to educate him in her business affairs. In due time he became a well-known trader in charge of the largest caravans. At twenty-six he married his employer, who was fifteen years older than he.

In 610, after fourteen years of marriage, Muhammad heard a voice speak to him; shortly thereafter he began to preach his newfound creed focusing on Allah and male dominion over nature and women. After twelve years of antagonizing his fellow men and women with his heretical ideas, he was cast out from his tribe, leaving Mecca on June 15, 622, an occasion that marks the first day of the Islamic calendar. His teachings fell on receiving ears among the men of Medina and the surrounding vicinity; he returned to

[*] The name Al'Lat simply means "goddess," similar to calling the Judeo-Christian god Jehovah, the Islamic god Allah, or both simply "God" or "the Lord."

[**] Sun, Moon, Mercury, Venus, Mars, Jupiter, and Saturn—the planets visible to the unaided human eye.

Mecca with an army of followers and conquered the city. Apparently tired of having his life ruled by women and goddesses, Muhammad destroyed all "false idols" of the sacred shrines, with the exception of the most holy, the sacred black stone that had once fallen from heaven.

Such pieces of meteorites that crashed through the atmosphere were regarded as true gifts from heaven, held in the highest esteem everywhere in the Near Eastern and Mediterranean cultures. Above all other things, it was the presence of the sacred black stone that made Mecca the place of power it was at the time.

By now a truly experienced leader and accepted prophet, Muhammad changed the divine name of Al'Lat into Allah.[*] By inventing his own history and mythology, he also transformed the Goddess's stone into a symbol of God—the right hand of Allah. Such a transformation of the Goddess into a male god figure certainly must have been unwanted by the general population. Muhammad also devised a way to incorporate into the Islamic code, and thus subjugate, the three aspects of Al'Lat. As is evidenced by a reading of the preface to the Koran, Islamic tradition now views these three as daughters of Allah.

There are those who claim that woman and the Goddess never had the exalted status in the Near East that I here state—scientists and scholars who simply cannot and will not admit that there has ever been a matriarchy in earlier human communities, and steadfastly state that goddesses have always played only a minor role in their respective pantheons. However, even from within the ranks of patriarchal observers we have witnesses for our case. An open and clear testimony to the fact that in pre-Islamic Arabia both the Goddess and women played a superior role can be found in the following statement by Omar, a faithful disciple of the prophet Muhammad. Omar states, "When we came among the Helpers, they proved to be a people whose women dominated them, and our wives have come to copy the habits of the women of the Ansar."[**]

After all this, what else can be said? In fact, there are a few more pieces of information to ponder. Is it perhaps significant that the Koran is written in Arabic as *Qur'an,* suggesting that the original title meant "the word of Qure"? Is it a coincidence that the priests who serve the shrine are still known today as *beni shaybah,* the "sons of the Old Woman"? Is it also a coincidence that Islamic pilgrims who visit the Kaaba during the hajj (see glossary) circle it seven times, just as did the nude worshipers of Al'Uzza?

In the final analysis, no one except the pilgrims themselves can know what they see and feel when finally arriving at the stone, the Yoni of the Goddess or a Hand of God. Whatever it may be, it is the most exalted aim of the pilgrimage to touch or to kiss the black meteorite.

FIGURE 56
This drawing by Christina Camphausen shows the inlaid black meteorite at the southeastern corner of the Kaaba.

---

[*] This is agreed upon by most non-Islamic sources. Author M. J. Vermaseren (see bibliography) points out that, grammatically, the name Allah is simply the male version of Al'Lat.
[**] Helpers is the name of the Ansar tribe of Medina.

▼

ULTIMATE EXPOSURE

The Valley Spirit never dies.
It is named the mysterious female.
And the doorway of the mysterious female
is the base from which
heaven and earth sprang.
It is there within us all the while;
draw upon it as you will,
it never runs dry.

TAO-TE CHING, 1:6.[1]

From Ireland to Japan, from Turkey to Ecuador, and from India to Australia, archeologists, anthropologists, and art historians worldwide have unearthed female figurines bearing more or less the same stance. These images would not shock or dismay the beholder if they showed a mother breast-feeding her child, a woman embracing a man, or a goddess blessing a crowd. The figurines I speak of, however, are much more powerful images, ones that have surprised and even offended many people. For not only are the women or deities represented in these sculptures completely nude, but each woman depicted in these figurines is actively exposing her Yoni, or her Heavenly Gate as the Chinese call it.

It is easy to imagine that these figurines have raised puritanical eyebrows. Many such images were hidden in museum cellars, explained away as strange and without significance. The few authors who have researched them▾ attempt to answer the question "Why? Why were these images produced?" rather than the more obvious question: "Why not?" No matter how serious these authors' intentions may have been or how brilliant some of their arguments may sound to a contemporary Christian or a present-day psychoanalyst, most researchers who have approached this topic have made the mistake of judging the value of these

▾ Notably Jørgen Andersen, and Anthony Weir and James Jerman—see bibliography.

images by the standards of their own time, rather than trying to understand the thoughts and feelings of an artisan who lived not only in a different time but by a totally different set of values.

Any society in which woman, the Goddess, and the Yoni were regarded as naturally powerful, naturally sacred, and naturally magical would spawn people who could hardly do anything else than display them in all fullness, power, and glory. Members of a society that reserved the concept of shame for true personal or communal failings rather than applying it to important and pleasurable parts of the body would find nothing disturbing or obscene in displaying what we call the "private parts." In a society free of sexual guilt and the interpretation of humanity's "original sin," artists, film producers, and art directors would display hundreds of Heavenly Gates to every one scene of violence, betrayal, racism, or chauvinism.

I am not claiming that human history has ever known a perfect society and, given the human condition, I doubt such a society will ever emerge. While I do believe that prehistoric peoples▾ had a healthy relationship to the physical body, there doubtless were other aspects of societal life that bespoke violence against self and others. I have no intention of degrading the past by romanticizing it; however, most of us well-informed modern women and men would do well to take off our socially dictated glasses and look at the past without interpreting it from the point of view of the present. This chapter, with its many images of so-called exhibitionist and obscene female figurines, is a good exercise in this new way of viewing.

Before we turn to the sculptures that have raised the ire of many a bishop, priest, and city council member, I would like to take the reader on a short trip to Japan. Not only does the mythology of that country include a story that focuses on a divine striptease dancer, and especially on the exposure of her Yoni, but the particular myth and its annual reenactment during the Kagura festival is mirrored in a peculiar stage act found nowhere

FIGURE 58
This ancestor spirit used to be part of the entrance to the ceremonial house for unmarried men in nineteenth-century Pulau, Micronesia.

FIGURE 59

Many medieval churches and monasteries in the British Isles and western Europe have so-called exhibitionist images such as this one from Kilsarkan, in the County of Kerry. It is evident from the continuing abrasion of the stones in the twentieth century that people do touch these images at or near the yoni. For a further discussion, see page 61.

else in the world. The evolution of this cultural story and practice gives us an interesting example of how, over time, a myth can change almost beyond recognition, yet with its essential meaning and intent remaining intact.

THE MYTHOLOGY OF STRIPTEASE

An old Shinto ritual celebrated annually in Japan includes the performance of a striptease in which the dancing priestess exposes her Yoni in full view of the participants. The Kagura ritual (J: "that which pleases the gods") commemorates an ancient myth concerning the goddesses Amaterasu and Ama-no-Uzume. In this story, public exhibition of the Yoni is used to initiate a process of change, both on an individual level—freeing Amaterasu of her self-imposed prison—and on a planetary scale—inviting the return of light and warmth necessary to the survival of life. There are distinct parallels between this story and the Greek myth involving Baubo, the exhibitionist maid of the goddess Demeter.

Amaterasu-o-mi-Kami (J: "Heaven Radiant Great Divinity"), the Shinto goddess of the sun and as such of light and life, had been sexually assaulted by her brother and was, quite naturally, deeply angered and depressed. Wounded, indignant, angry, and in pain, she left the world; wanting no part of it any longer, she took to hiding in a cave, thus withholding light and warmth from the earth and all humanity. Realizing the dangers involved, other deities assembled and tried to convince Amaterasu to come out again and shine, but their supplications were to no avail. After several attempts to persuade the sun to come out of hiding, it was Ama-no-Uzume, the Dread Female of Heaven, whose idea lured Amaterasu out of hiding. Ama-no-Uzume positioned herself in front of all the assembled deities and

Ultimate Exposure

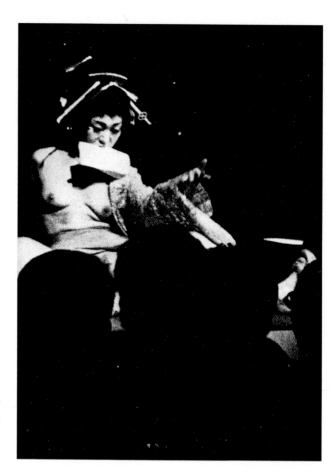

Figure 60
*A Japanese woman and her
peering spectators during a
performance of the tokudashi in
the red-light district of Tokyo.*

began to dance the dance of life. Enticed by her charms, everyone except Amaterasu watched Ama-no-Uzume's performance. Once Ama-no-Uzume knew that she had everyone's undivided attention, she lifted her skirt and exposed her Yoni for all to see. The people in the assemblage roared with laughter and clapped their hands, and the noise carried far, all the way to the cave of the Sun Goddess. Curious about the ruckus, curious at how anyone could be joyful while darkness had fallen, Amaterasu left her hiding place, coming out of her cave to be once more among the living. Once again, there was light.

It is this beautiful myth of a divine striptease that has given rise to the Japanese Kagura ritual, a ritual that has been enacted every year since the dawn of memory in a celebration during which a human priestess plays the part of Ama-no-Uzume, and in which the audience consists not of deities but of an assembly of faithful temple visitors. Exhibition of the Yoni has become so deeply embedded in Japanese culture that its basic content is still operative even in a nonmythical, nonreligious, and more or less pornographic context. The sacred Kagura ritual laid the groundwork for the profane *tokudashi*, another kind of ritual that is regularly staged in some of the more luxurious erotic shows and striptease parlors in Kyoto, Tokyo, and elsewhere in Japan.

This remnant of the ancient Kagura has been described from firsthand observation in

Ian Buruma's nonfiction work *Behind the Mask*. Prudent imagery (photographs) of this event can be found in *Behind the Mask*, as well as in Lo Duca's work on Far Eastern eroticism (see bibliography for both).

As suggested in the excerpts that follow, the tokudashi seems to be a modern remnant of the ancient custom of publicly worshiping the female genitals, a custom now heavily veiled and yet certainly not forgotten. This shrouding of yoni-worshiping customs is especially strange in terms of Japan, however, as it is one of the few countries in which people from all ranks of society still engage in overt phallic worship in an annual celebration so public that it is reported on by the major media. In the Matsuri celebration all participants, including women and children, carry phalluses as good luck charms; at the height of the celebration, each person touches and kisses a huge phallus while praying that his or her wishes be fulfilled.

While early Japanese sculpture indicates that Yoni worship was widely practiced in the past, it seems that practices venerating the Yoni have gone underground, becoming part of the sex industry in the form of tokudashi. However, while the cultural context and the setting of the original ritual have changed radically, the tokudashi is essentially a modern continuance of the old Japanese Kagura. It is noteworthy that the authors of the following extracts describing the tokudashi refer to the women onstage as matriarchal goddesses or maternal queens, and the Yoni as the magical organ or inner sanctum, terms that hardly ever appear in the context of sex shows.

Ian Buruma *(Behind the Mask)* describes the tokudashi like this:

> The girls shuffle over to the edge of the stage, crouch and, leaning back as far as they can, slowly open their legs just a few inches from the flushed faces in the front row. The audience … leans forward to get a better view of this mesmerizing sight, this magical organ, revealed in all its mysterious glory. The women … slowly move around, crablike, from person to person, softly encouraging the spectators to take a closer look. To aid the men in their explorations, they hand out magnifying glasses and small hand-torches, which pass from hand to hand. All the attention is focused on that one spot of the female anatomy; instead of being the humiliated objects of masculine desire, these women seem in complete control, like matriarchal goddesses.

A similar account, written with more literary imagination, can be found in the opening scene of *White Ninja* by Eric van Lustbader, the author of several best-selling novels combining Eastern philosophy, martial arts, and sexuality. In this scene, a Japanese man by the name of Senjin visits a club called the Silk Road; the entrance to the club is described as resembling "the inner petals of an enormous orchid":

> Eventually the girls emerged [onto the stage]. They wore oddly demure robes that covered them from throat to ankle so that they had the aspect of oracles or sibyls from whose mouth the fates of the men in the audience would soon be made manifest.

Apart from their faces, one could not see what they looked like at all. One had, rather, to trust those gently smiling faces that looked like neither angel or vixen, but were suffused with such a maternal glow that it was impossible to find them intimidating or frightening. Senjin concentrated his attention on one of the girls, the one closest to him. She was as startlingly young as she was beautiful. He licked his lips as if he was about to sit down to a long awaited feast.

The music had changed. It was clankier now, more obviously sexual in its beat and in the insinuation of the brass arrangement. The girls simultaneously untied their robes, let them slip to the Plexiglas stage. They wore various forms of street clothes, most of them suggestive in one way or another. Strobe lights flashed. In unison the girls began to strip, not in any Western bump-and-grind fashion, but in a series of still-life tableaux, freeze frame images held on the video of the mind. The poses, as the garments came off, were increasingly wanton, until, at length, the girls were naked.

The music died with most of the light, and Senjin could hear a restive stirring in the audience. The scent of sweat outmuscled all others now. The girl in front of Senjin had flawless skin. Her muscles had the firmness, the roundness of youth. Her small breasts stood out almost straight from her body, and the narrow line of her pubic hair would have revealed more than it concealed were it not deftly hidden in shadow.

Now the girl squatted down. In her hands were fistfuls of tiny flashlights imprinted with the name of the club, the Silk Road. She offered one to Senjin, who refused. But immediately there was a mad scramble over his back, as the businessmen lunged to grab flashlights from her hands.

When the flashlights were gone, the girl bent her upper torso backward until her nipples pointed up at the mirrored ceiling where they were replicated over and over. Balancing herself on her heels as deftly as an acrobat, the dancer began to part her legs. This was the climax of her act, the *tokudashi*, colloquially known in leering double entendre as "the open."

Senjin could hear the clicking all around him as the tiny flashlights came on, insect eyes in a field of heaving wheat. He was sure that every man in the club was concentrating on that one spot between the girl's legs. The flashlight beams probed into those inner sanctums as the girls moved about the stage, keeping their legs remarkably wide open.

Senjin watched the muscles in the girl's legs bunch and move as she slowly scuttled around the entire perimeter of the stage as easily as if she were a contortionist in a circus. All the while, her face was serene and in control as if she were a queen or a goddess under whose spell these mortals had come. As long as she held her legs apart, for the most minute inspection, this girl, and the others above and around her, maintained a magnetic power as hard to explain as it was to define.

The lights came on abruptly, dazzlingly, breaking the hushed florid silence. The rock music blared anew, the girls reclothed in their robes, once again mysterious, their faces now devoid of any emotion or involvement.

THE YONI AS MAGICAL INSTRUMENT

The Japanese myth of exposing the Yoni to influence someone or something stands not alone in the world. Other myths and practices are known to exist in a variety of cultures. Similar in intent and yet different in detail, they depict the Yoni as having powers beyond all else.

Concerning the magical effects of nudity in general and of exposing the sexual organs in particular, the ancient stories of a variety of peoples suggest that the genitals—especially those of women—exude an inherent magnetic force. Such myths and legends show clearly that our ancestors of cultures past regarded the Yoni as a kind of magical weapon imbued with protective and healing energies and believed that the exhibition of the Yoni has the power to effect certain magical spells. Not only was flashing the Yoni at the devil regarded as a fail-safe method to hinder his approach (see figure 61), but in more general terms, it was seen as a means to avert evil forces in general.

The high esteem in which the people of earlier civilizations, from Greece and Egypt to Africa, India, and the Pacific Islands, held this yoni power is well documented. Both Pliny (23–79 C.E.) and Plutarch (46–126 C.E.), trusted historians of the ancient world, reported that even great heroes and gods had to flee from the sight of the naked Yoni. Many of the nude and erotic sculptures at the temple of Khajuraho in India show both women

FIGURE 61
This drawing by Charles Eisen of a woman scaring the devil by lifting her skirt depicts the widespread belief in the protective powers of the Yoni.

FIGURE 62
One finds the motif of a woman exposing herself to dispel evil in Asia as well as in Europe and Africa. This twentieth-century wooden female guardian is carved into a door in Timor, Indonesia.

Ultimate Exposure

and men exposing or exhibiting their genitals; here too such exposure was thought to dispel evil influences. As well, women in the southern Indian province of Madras were known to expose themselves in order to quiet dangerous storms.

Egyptian women exposed their yonis in order to drive away evil spirits from their fields; a similar intent is suggested by a number of Theban wall paintings. The custom was also known farther south. Briffault, in his three-volume collection of facts and tales from the past,[2] tells of a sixteenth-century traveler to Africa who reported that even a wild lion was thought to shy away from the sight of a naked Yoni.

It is important to note that in the preceding examples, the yonic energy that is used to dispel evil forces, avert disaster, or banish unwelcome guests originates not in supernatural beings but in ordinary women. The Yoni power displayed in these stories and images is the natural heritage of every woman.

To be certain, legends also exist in which it is the Divine Yoni from whence such magnetic energy is derived. In these cases, the Yoni is seen not so much as a protecting or guarding force but as one that actively provides for and nourishes an individual or a whole group of people. One such story is expressed in a rock painting found in Tassili, in the Sahara. The painting, dating back to c. 8000–5000 B.C.E., shows a hunter stalking his prey. A power line runs from the Yoni of a woman/Goddess to the hunter and his weapon. This work has sometimes been classified as an expression of hunting magic, imparting a focus that disregards the main image of this piece of religious art: The rock painting shows that the magical force flowing from the Yoni bestows the Great Mother's permission upon the hunter and his weapon that the prey may be killed. The picture says, in fact, that the taking of life can be granted only by the one who is also able to create life.

A story from eighth-century Tibet tells of the power of a goddess's Yoni relative to the concept of initiation. The story also shows that, despite the air of male domination that has crept into Tibetan Buddhism, the principal initiator into the Buddhist mysteries is Woman. The story is especially important in that it concerns Padmasambhava (c. 730–805), an early Tantric adept and magician who is highly venerated in Tibet as a foremost

Figure 63
The relationship between Goddess, hunter, and prey is shown in this ancient rock painting from Tassili in the Sahara.

FIGURES 64 AND 65
Two examples of statues depicting Baubo, the personified Yoni. These Near Eastern terra-cotta figures are from Priene and date back to the fifth century B.C.E.

agent in bringing Buddhism and Tantra from India to the Himalayas. The legends surrounding Padmasambhava characterize him as a semidivine and ultimately powerful being who almost single-handedly freed Tibet from the demons of its past (the deities of pre-Buddhist shamanism). Padmasambhava's rank in the Tibetan Buddhist nobility is second only to that of the Buddha himself.

In his secret biography,[3] Padmasambhava's principal lover and friend relates that this great guru's special knowledge and powers were gained by initiations from a powerful female adept or deity known as the dakini▾ Suryacandrasiddhi, whom Padmasambhava "begged for her teachings; outer, inner and secret" ones.[4] Giving in to his begging, the Great Sovereign Dakini actually swallows the hero. After being initiated and imbued with new magical powers, he is "ejected through her secret lotus."[5] The "secret lotus" is, of course, her Yoni.

Different in content yet certainly related to the same sense of Yoni power is the myth of Baubo▾▾ and Demeter. In this story of Demeter and her servant, Baubo spontaneously and unexpectedly raises her skirt and makes Demeter view her thus exposed Yoni.

After reading about the myth of Amaterasu and the Japanese striptease, you might

---

▾ Similarly to *yogini*, the term *dakini* is used to describe a category of goddesses or female initiates.
▾▾ Baubo originally was an Anatolian (present-day Turkey) goddess who was adopted by the Greeks.

FIGURE 66
Most famous among all the sheelas is
this stunning stone carving from the
church at Kilpeck, Herefordshire.
By opening her vulva as wide as
possible, this figure seems to show us
where we come from and, perhaps, to
invite us back into her womb once
life comes to an end.

ask "So what is new?" The truly interesting part of the story of Baubo and Demeter is the fact that this act of Yoni exposure does not happen in a setting of gaiety, erotic stimulation, or drunkenness but in a moment of utter despair and sadness—a moment in which Demeter, the fertile mother form of the great Mediterranean Triple Goddess, is in deep pain over the loss of her daughter, Kore. The virgin Kore has been raped and abducted into the netherworld by the god Pluto. Depressed and angry over her daughter's abduction, Demeter refuses to cooperate any longer in bringing fecundity to the world. As the Greek version of the Earth Mother, Demeter is responsible for and in charge of all fertility; without her active efforts and cooperation, grain will not grow and so the people will have no food.

On seeing Baubo's Secret Lotus, her Inner Sanctum, her Matrix of Creation—on seeing Baubo actually pointing at her Yoni—the weeping Demeter reaches spontaneous enlightenment and bursts into a liberating laughter, signaling her understanding and, simultaneously, the end of her withdrawal. With Demeter back from her self-imposed grief, life goes on.

The story of Baubo and her skirt-raising gesture has been researched by two very different yet equally insightful authors; both authors—one woman and one man[6]—have reached similar conclusions. According to these authors, Baubo's exhibitionist action is intended as a reminder to the grief-stricken Demeter that she—as woman and especially as the goddess of fertility—carries in herself the means to birth new life. Demeter's attachment and pain concerning her daughter, now abducted into the realm of Pluto, the Greek god of death, makes her forget her own creative power. Baubo's sudden action reminds Demeter that being a woman, having a Yoni, gives her the power to endlessly create new life. It is as if Baubo is saying "Being a woman, having a Yoni, we know life is temporary by definition; we know that all life will someday return to the womb of the Earth in an endless and unceasing cycle of transformation and rebirth." The stories of both the Japanese Ama-no-Uzume and the European Baubo show clearly what powers were once ascribed to the exposure of that which alone can create.

To the ancient Greeks, wise old Baubo became the Yoni personified. Little did they know that centuries later, even after Christianity had begun to hold sway over most peoples of Europe, Baubo would be faced with serious competition from the many images of nude women/deities that have been found on the walls of churches and monasteries in Celtic lands.

Sheela-na-gig is the collective name for the female figurines found in western Europe, mainly in the region of present-day Ireland, but also in neighboring countries such as England, Scotland, France, and Germany. The sheelas are mostly cut from stone and show a standing, squatting, or reclining female figure with legs spread wide, fully exposing her Yoni.

Little is known of the background and ritual purpose of these sculptures; we there-

FIGURES 67 AND 68
Two variations of the sheela motif. The example on the left, from France, is exceptional in that, the figure is reclining and has full breasts. The figure at right is unique because of the exaggerated size of her genitals. This sheela from England almost looks like a stone-carved version of the large-lipped All Mother from Australia (see page 4).

Ultimate Exposure

fore must approach this topic with both a mythographic and an intuitive mind. As Jørgen Andersen suggests,[7] it may well be that the sheelas also served as protectors and guardians, keeping evil influences—especially from sacred places such as churches and nunneries—at bay. If one considers the sheelas to be basically exhibitionist, they may have a connection to such legendary figures as Baubo and Ama-no-Uzume.

As an object of meditation on the endless cycle of birth and death, these sculptures show an interesting parallel to the women or images at the center of a Tantric Yoni Puja (see chapter 4). This particular association seems especially plausible when we realize that the term *Sheela-na-gig* has always been a considerable puzzle to etymologists, considering that it seems unrelated to any of the languages ever spoken in the British Isles.[▼] At the temple at Erech in Mesopotamia, the term *nu-gug*, "the pure and immaculate ones," was used to designate priestesses who held the office of sacred harlot and thus performed temple prostitution. It is therefore possible that the sheelas represent a Celtic or pre-Celtic version of Oriental and Mediterranean sacred prostitutes, suggesting that they may have been imported from the East.

▼ An observation by Brian Branston (see bibliography), waving aside Victorian explanations of the term as meaning "lewd women."

The explanation of the origin and purpose of the sheelas put forward by Anthony Weir and James Jerman[8] is the least plausible. Driven by a personal need to deny all divine ancestry for the sheelas, the authors argue that these images were created by the medieval masons as constant warnings against sins of the flesh. This interpretation, however, is not at all convincing, not only because distinctly similar images have been found in regions and cultures where no Christian has ever trod ground, but also because local communities have been known to demand that sheelas that were removed by local clergy be reinstalled. As well, even today a great many people—outwardly Christians perhaps, but inwardly bound to more ancient traditions—continue to touch these figures at the Yoni, the place of power. Such public engagement shows that local folklore held these figures in high regard.

Images similar to the sheelas appear in South America, the Near East, India, and Oceania (see page 51 and pages 52, 57, and 62). Given what we know about the ancients' regard for the power of the exposed Yoni, the pervasiveness of the sheela-na-gig images suggests that they too belong to the tradition of Goddess and Yoni worship.

6

▽

RAJAS: BLOOD OF CREATION, NECTAR OF PASSION[*]

Blessed be Thy womb, without which we would not be.

FROM A WICCAN INCANTATION

One aspect of Tantra that has made it a supreme teaching is the fact that, during its early development, women were strongly involved in the shaping of its tenets, principles, and practices. The women who were so instrumental in the early development of Tantra were most often not mothers, married women, or cloistered nuns, whose lives (then, as now) got all too easily tied up by multiple responsibilities and social expectations. Instead, these women who influenced the Tantric religion led independent lives filled with traveling, learning, teaching, and experimenting with the Tantric practices.

Within the Tantric teachings there is no doubt that women have the ability to and indeed can be leaders of all kinds, including religious leaders; likewise, there is no doubt that women possess libido or that women do, in fact, ejaculate. In short, there is no doubt that women are beings of power. When one compares this informed and

▼ *Rajas*, a word from the sacred language commonly known as Sanskrit, is an ambiguous term and therefore difficult to define. In mainstream Hinduism, rajas is one of the three basic qualities or properties (S: *guna*; see glossary) that permeate all of creation. In regard to our present inquiry, the term *rajas* also refers to the various types of secretions or fluids originating in or emanating from the yoni. But even within such a clearly delineated field, *rajas* can refer to two very different things. The term refers to the monthly menstrual fluid created by women between menarche and menopause; the term also refers to the juices of passion produced in and by the yoni when it is aroused. The attribution of "red" in describing this nectar of passion is not meant to be taken literally; it simply contrasts female ejaculate (red semen) with male ejaculate (white semen).

enlightened stance regarding women with the disparaging views generally held by present-day scientific or religious authorities, one wonders why these people are still in office and why we pay their salaries. But we all know why: we live in a still thoroughly patriarchal world.

The world of Tantra and Shakta (see glossary for both) is a completely different one, one in which positive role models for women abound. The Tantric pantheon has more goddesses, female teachers, woman initiates, and female adepts of the magical and sexual arts than any other religion on this planet. One reason for this is the strong female influence that helped shape Tantra.[▾]

Another reason lies in the fact that, because of the interdependence of male and female practitioners in performing the actual techniques, often sexual in nature, the two genders developed ways to relate with each other that were intimate, consenting, noncoercive, nonpossessive, and mutually beneficial. This recasting of the female/male relationship is a far cry from the war between genders and the unbearable heaviness of being that is experienced in many contemporary relationships formed under Christian, Jewish, Islamic, Hindu, Buddhist, or any other system that promotes limited conceptions of the respective roles and values of women and men.

As suggested in my definition of the term *rajas,* Tantra speaks not only of a male, white semen but of a red, female equivalent. It is important to realize that this ejaculate is not regarded as figurative or symbolic; it is regarded quite literally. In fact, the Sanskrit word used for both male and female semen is *sukra.* Is it not interesting that in the India of centuries past, women and men seem to have been regarded as equal even on that level?

I will speak about the sexual secretions of the yoni later in the chapter. Let us first turn our attention to the type of rajas that is not produced by both genders: the menstrual fluid. Unique to women, this powerful liquid has often been feared, has sometimes been imitated, and yet has been regarded by most cultures as unimportant or unclean.

THE MENSTRUATING YONI

A specialized expression of Yoni magic can be recognized in the range of immense powers that people of various cultures have attributed to the monthly menstrual fluid, and especially to the first blood, the blood that signals a girl's transformation into a woman. A wealth of material has been published on the many taboos surrounding menstruation. Menstrual fluid was said to have negative effects on other humans, animals, and nature. Menstruating women were separated from tribe and family for fear of contamination—they were made to stay clear of places where bread was baked or food was prepared or kings would tread. These injunctions and hundreds like them,[▾▾] changing from culture

---

[▾] Despite many published misunderstandings, this is obvious to anyone actually practicing its teachings, but it also has now been carefully researched and convincingly explained by Miranda Shaw in her book Passionate Enlightenment.

[▾▾] For more detailed examples consult the bibliography under Briffault, Delaney, Chris Knight, Lander, Owen, Shuttle, and Dena Taylor.

Figure 72
In this drawing, Moonflower, *Dutch artist Christina Camphausen illustrates the Sanskrit term yonipuspa ("vulva flower") in which menstruation is regarded as the flowering of the Yoni in tune with the phases of the moon.*

to culture and across time, make clear the degree to which it was believed that the menstrual fluid was infused with unique powers, even if they were regarded as harmful.

There are, however, other examples of peoples who held the menstrual fluid in high regard. Although this is especially true of Tantra and Shakta, there are examples from cultures outside this sphere. Some of those include the following:

* Among the Incas, the moon goddess Mama Kilya, responsible for all cyclic phenomena of nature, was worshiped as the ruler of the menstrual cycle.

* Among alchemists, the potent energy of menstrual blood was recognized by the name *elixir rubeus* (L: "red elixir"). This elixir was thought to be most powerful when generated during the full moon.

* Among adepts of certain schools of left-handed Tantra (see glossary), drinking yonipuspa (S: "vulva flower"), the menstrual fluid, is regarded as a sure means of reaching liberation.

* In ancient Persia, the goddess Jaki was thought to be responsible for menstruation. In later patriarchal times, when menstruation took on negative connotations, Jaki became a demon said to urge men to evil deeds.

- In ancient Egypt, people wore amulets of red stone that represented or imparted the powers inherent in the mentrual blood of Isis, the most prominent of all Egyptian goddesses.

- Folklore also attests to the same basic belief in the magic of menstrual blood. In Calabria, Italy, for example, women used to save a few drops of their menstrual fluid in a small bottle that they carried wherever they went. When such drops were secretly administered to a man of their choice, it was believed that the man would be bound to them forever.

Before we take a closer look at how menstrual fluid is regarded and used in India, we should also realize that Indians were not alone in their use of this and other products of the Yoni. Among certain Gnostic sects there existed a similar insight about the powers inherent in the types of rajas (female secretions). As reported by Epiphanus of Salamis (315–403), both the juices of love and the menstrual fluid were treated with reverence, being ritually collected and then used in religious rituals.

Tantra and Shakta are among the very few religious systems in which menstruation is not seen as unclean or dangerous or something to be hidden. On the contrary, in many Tantric sects, and especially in Shakta, the menstrual taboo of mainstream Indian society is recognized as simply another aspect of general human ignorance. In this sense, the menstrual taboo is not "broken down" in these religions, as suggested by Ajit Mookerjee;[1] the taboo simply does not exist. For men and women who regard menstrual fluid as sacred and worthy of veneration, the time of menstruation is a special one, and a woman whose blood is flowing is valued and honored. In ritual practice such as the Yoni Puja, a menstruating woman has a very special place, not only because of the different quality of her energy at this time[2] but also quite simply because of the blood itself, the unique and magical moon-blood that is the property and power of woman. Therefore, when left-handed Tantrics mingle menstrual fluid with wine and take it as a ritual drink, or kiss the Yoni during puja instead of only touching it, they likely reenact a ritual that is nearly as old as Homo sapiens, a ritual that probably took place 25,000 years ago in the special Yoni chambers of the paleolithic caves.

Many Indian authors, however, are inwardly ashamed of such aspects of their heritage; they therefore hardly ever say all that could be said about Yoni worship in Indian culture. For example, in his book *Goddess Cults in Ancient India,* Jagdish Tiwari states that the ancient Greeks are responsible for the nude, squatting figures of India. We encounter a similar sense of need to play down the truth when Ajit Mookerjee says that "in Kerala a ceremony called *trippukharattu* is held eight or ten times a year. At these periods a reddened cloth wrapped around the image of the goddess is keenly sought after by pilgrims and prized as a holy relic."[3] What is being said here is only a small part of the truth. The author does not tell us how or with what the cloth that becomes a holy relic is so reddened. To admit that the cloth is colored by the blood of menstruating women (or if that goes too far for the local community, with the blood of a sacrificed animal) is apparently too offensive for the author, or at least for the (mostly Western) readership that he and his

FIGURE 73
The Egyptian symbol theth is a stylized representation of the goddess Isis's vulva. When worn as an amulet, the symbol was believed to confer the powers of the blood of Isis, Egypt's most exalted goddess. (Also see the image on page 64.)

Rajas

FIGURE 74
This beautiful wood carving from
southern India shows a woman
menstruating, most likely during a
ritual celebration in which this
specific female energy was both
venerated and absorbed by the
practitioners.

publisher envision. In this case as in many others, the information that truly shows how her worshipers look upon women, the Yoni, and menstrual fluid is withheld, even by an author who appears to be open about the sexual aspects of religion and ritual.▼

The practices that take place all over India in those areas where people live according to the precepts of Tantra or Shakta go much further than regarding an artificially reddened cloth as a holy relic. In fact, Yoni worshipers—male and female, young and old—make their holy relics with the real and living blood that flows from a menstruating woman. With the blood from the Yoni of a previously consecrated woman, the priest first paints a triangle on her shaved pubic mound. Once this is accomplished, an absorbent

▼ I would like to state here that I have no quarrel with Mookerjee and no intention to denigrate his work. Without his efforts much information about the sacred in Indian culture would still be unknown to us, and I am grateful to him for his work.

piece of cloth or paper is pressed to the woman's pubic area, and a print of the triangle is thus made. Such dried prints are found in the private homes and secret temples of her worshipers, where they serve as objects of meditation and veneration.

The Bauls of Bengal are another group of people for whom menstruation is an occasion for joy and celebration rather than segregation, shame, or fear. We know about Baul practice mainly through the writing of Bhaskar Bhattacharyya, an initiated Baul, in conjunction with Nik Douglas and Penny Slinger.[4] The Bauls, a people comparable to the mystic minstrels of the European Middle Ages, live according to a philosophy that combines elements of the Tantric tradition with those of mainstream Hinduism. They are especially devoted to the female deity Radha and the male Krishna. The time of menstruation is regarded by these people as auspicious and powerful indeed.

The Bauls roam their home country in eastern India. Through their songs of love and devotion they spread the word that communion with the Divine can be achieved with the help of the body—by ritual, by sexual union, and especially by making use of the forces inherent in the menstrual fluid. For this reason the Bauls rarely practice their sexual rituals at times other than the three and one-half days of the menstrual period.

As might be expected from a people embedded in a tradition so intently focused on this aspect of the female, the Bauls have developed a rather specialized knowledge concerning menstruation. According to Baul teachings, menstrual fluid is of varying types depending on the time of the cycle. The Bauls equate these types of blood with the three sacred rivers in Indian tradition: the Ganges, the Sarasvati, and the Jamuna. "Jamuna, the dark one, flows during the initial stage of menstruation, followed by Sarasvati, the red fluid, and Ganga, the light-colored fluid. Each type of menstrual secretion takes 24 hours to manifest itself fully.... During the final half day the menstrual secretion starts to ebb."[5]

The Baul's monthly ritual, eighty-four hours filled with music and song, passion and devotion, is known as "manifesting the full moon at the time of the new moon," and its final aim is to "catch the uncatchable," the unique energy possessed only by women. This energy is said to manifest during the last twelve-hour phase of menstruation. By union with a menstruating woman during that time, a man can also partake of the Goddess's powers, distributed to him by way of a consenting female partner.

Would not all of us benefit from such a manner of looking at women and their unique powers, rather than regarding menstruation as a curse, as unclean, or as something to be hidden, sometimes even from loved ones? Certainly it will not be easy, and it may not even be possible, to change the views of mainstream society concerning these matters. What is possible, however, is to change our own views and to personally challenge the taboo that has been imposed on us by parents (who usually did not know better), peers (the wrong ones), and popes (who have never understood anything about women).

It is not only in Indian Tantra that we find reverence for and ritual use of menstrual fluids. Such practices have also been documented within Tibetan Tantra.▾ Despite the fact that contemporary Tibetan lamas, even more so than Indian adepts, are usually quite

▾ This religious system is sometimes called esoteric Tibetan Buddhism, Buddhist Tantra, or Vajrayana.

secretive about the sexual aspects of their teachings, other people—in their translations of original Tibetan documents—feel less constrained. For example, Keith Dowman, in his translation of the Tibetan text *The Secret Life and Songs of the Lady Yeshe Tsogyal*, translates a passage that unmistakably reveals the high regard ancient Tantric adepts had for the powers of the menstrual flow. In this passage one of the religion's cofounders, the high female adept and teacher Yeshe Tsogyal (757–817), reports one of her extraordinary visions as follows: "Then I had a vision of a red woman, naked, lacking even the covering of bone ornaments, who thrust her *bhaga* [yoni; see glossary] against my mouth; and I drank deeply from her copious flow of blood."[6]

In this statement from an ancient and revered text, not only is the drinking of the menstrual blood from the Yoni spoken of directly; but also the text shows that such practice seems not to have been restricted to heterosexual couples, as is all too often assumed by anyone thinking or writing about these matters. However, the text should not be overzealously interpreted to mean that Yeshe Tsogyal preferred to practice her sexual rituals with women rather than men. In a biography Yeshe Tsogyal wrote about Padmasambhava (730–805), the man who is officially credited with having brought Tantra and Buddhism to Tibet, she speaks clearly of how she went into retreat with two male adepts. The rituals they practiced there (as did and do many others) are known in Tibet as *zap-lam* (see glossary) and as "the path of relying upon the body of another person," a teaching that was mainly transmitted by a woman, the eleventh-century initiate known in Tibet as Vajradhara Niguma and in India as Yogini Vimalashri.

With this short excursion into some of the truly sexual practices that belong to both Indian and Tibetan Tantra, we leave the topic of menstruation. Much more could be said here about the motivation behind the various sexual practices and their psychosomatic benefits. However, as this is a book about the Yoni, not a book about sexuality as such, we will keep our focus honed. In the preceding pages, we have looked at the type of rajas that is menstruation. Now we will see what uses are made of the other rajas—sexual secretions—and the powers believed to be inherent in them.

THE ART OF NOURISHMENT

In addition to menstrual fluids, sexual secretions have also played an important part in the lives, sexual practices, and cultural concepts concerning women. Sometimes such secretions, or "juices of love," have been imbibed directly from the source by means of oral-genital contact, a sexual technique better known as cunnilingus. This term is a combination of the Latin words for vulva (L: *cunnus*) and tongue (L: *lingus*). Although this definition severely confines the imagination in terms of possible activities, in reality the term is more broadly applied. The technique includes using lips and teeth as well as the tongue, with stimulation not being limited to the vulva but also including the clitoris and the opening to the vagina. In Sanskrit, one is more realistic and calls all of these activities by the word *auparishtaka* (S: mouth congress). Apart from being enjoyed by a countless unknown number of people across time and cultures, cunnilingus was and is held in high

FIGURE 75
A Yoni-shaped insignia and amulet worn in the circles of the secret society A∴A∴ of The Hague, Netherlands, founded in 1929. Members of the society practiced sexual magic. Judging from their documents, cunnilingus seems to have been one their favorite techniques.

regard among certain Tantric groups, among Chinese adepts and Chinese royalty, and among members of various secret societies in Europe and the United States, brotherhoods and sisterhoods practicing what is often called sexual magic.▾

To the adepts of sexual ritual and practice, cunnilingus was not the only way of drinking the divine nectar; the same nectar could be generated and drunk by other means. It is here that the Taoist, Tantric, and sex-magic arts and methods of semen retention come into play, although the practices are based on different motivations. In China, for instance, the man would not ejaculate in order to not lose any of his precious energies; female ejaculation in China, though, was valued all the more. Although this process is often called "dual cultivation," it rarely seems designed to benefit both partners equally. The Chinese sex magicians, emperors, and adepts knew all too well that they would be nourished and revitalized by the secretions of the Yoni, and usually that is all they wanted. To the ancient Chinese, ever concerned with longevity and virility, the yin essence (C: *yin-ching*) from the Palace of Yin (C: *yin-kung*) was one of the most beneficent substances a man could absorb from a woman. The Chinese were so fascinated by the beneficial substances in all female secretions that they considered the mouth (or lips), the breasts, and the Yoni to each be one peak described in the term *medicine of the three peaks* (C: *san-feng*).

A similar science of secretions, developed in India, is concerned with both the female

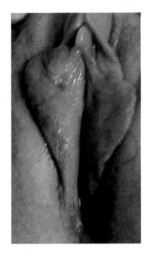

FIGURE 76
An aroused yoni glistening with yin essence.

▾ When *magic* is spelled with a k, as in magick, it shows the group to be affiliated with or deriving from the teachings of Aleister Crowley

Rajas

and the male varieties. One of the disciplines of *sri vidya* (S: "knowledge of the Goddess") is the study of all human secretions generated by erotic, sexual, and reproductive activity and of the subtle, energetic components that are an intrinsic part of these secretions.

As described in chapter 4, some Tantric rituals are designed to mingle male and female juices, which are then imbibed. Other rituals are especially designed to stimulate the production of female secretions only. In such cases the officiating adept will stimulate the woman, recognized as the representative of the Goddess, by all means, including *maithuna* (S: "ritual intercourse"). However, he "must not let his own seed fall"; the aim of the ritual is to collect the female sexual fluids, which are then "placed in a conch shell half filled with purificatory water and half with wine."[7] Finally, after many more ritual steps have been undertaken, the mixture of water, wine, and female juices is used to purify other offerings. The remaining liquid is then drunk by the congregation.

The specific ritual described here belongs to those that form the body of the worship of Kali, perhaps the most popular goddess in all of India. The iconography of Kali, the Great Goddess of life and death, is most interesting. Very often she is shown in sexual union with the god Shiva, who is lying on his back, the goddess riding his erect lingam.

This stance clearly indicates that it is he who receives her, and that it is she who is the dynamic force, the true essence. Shiva receives her juices (the divine essence), not the other way around. He, lying there as a corpse, is the passive and quiet equivalent of consciousness, whereas she, Kali, is the dynamic force of the universe, generating all creation and dissolution and recreation.

We are often and perhaps deliberately misled by so-called authorities who translate the sacred scriptures of the religions here discussed. I am disappointed by the lack of scientific objectivity shown by such authorities when, for example, I read a passage from David Snellgrove's translation of the Hevajra Tantra, one of the most sacred and basic texts of Tibetan Tantric Buddhism, that speaks of "concentrating the essence of woman"[8] where it should perhaps otherwise read "absorbing the female vaginal fluids."[9] Even if Snellgrove truly believes that his translation is the more correct or better one, many among his readership would expect him to clearly state a viable alternative rather than leaving it unmentioned. However, Mr. Snellgrove is not alone in such omissions that are aimed to obscure and hide the many sexual dimensions of Tantric Buddhism. It is a pity, but this concealment has become a rather common practice, one that makes it necessary to inquire personally into or wait for a second opinion on any text so translated.

A similar case of such dispute over translation has lately befallen the famous Tao-te Ching, the most basic text of Taoism by the legendary Chinese philosopher Lao Tzu (sixth century B.C.E.). The dispute concerns the meaning of a particular Chinese ideogram that is part of the quote reprinted at the beginning of chapter 5 (page 51). According to the native Chinese author Chou Tz'u-Chi, the newly discovered silken manuscript of this ancient document, having been found among the Ma-wang Tui texts,▼ does not use the ideogram "valley" but the ideogram "desire aroused by looking at the female genitals." Western sinologists, however, do not like to attribute such lustful words in a sacred text to the semidivine Lao Tzu, and remain adamant that the ideogram in question "can hardly mean anything other than valley or valley stream."[10] However, in consideration of the context in which the ideogram appears, the age of the text in question, and the pervasiveness of Yoni worship around the world at that time, the new insight makes sense. If the alternative ideogram is substituted, the quote in question reads as follows:

FIGURE 78
Based on the Chinese yin-yang symbol, this drawing by Christina Camphausen is a fully female interpretation and is therefore called Yin Yin.

The desire aroused by seeing the Yoni never dies.
It [the yoni] is named the mysterious female,
and the doorway of the mysterious female
is the base from which heaven and earth sprang.
It is there with us all the while.
Draw upon it as you will; it never runs dry.

▼ These texts are so named because of their discovery in the tomb of King Ma (second century B.C.E.). Apart from the oldest extant Tao-te Ching, the cache also includes several manuals concerned with the art of the bedchamber (see Wile in the bibliography), and a complete I Ching.

Rajas

This reading of the opening quote of the Tao-te Ching reminds us of Baubo, who presented Demeter with the the sight of the inner sanctum from which heaven and earth—and all else—is generated.

A final note is required at the end of this chapter, a note directed especially to those who would eagerly and perhaps all too thoughtlessly embark on a personal quest for the essence spoken of in this chapter. It must be clearly understood that in all such matters concerning the exchange of subtle energies between two or more partners, nothing can be received without the other partner actively and knowingly giving. In order for Tantric, Taoist, or Western sex-magic rituals to be useful and beneficial to anyone, each of the partners has to be aware of what is going on—each has to share the concepts, visualizations, consciousness, and wisdom. In other words, each has to be either initiated or particularly experienced, mature, and talented. If the woman whose rajas is being absorbed by her partner does not know about giving or does not want to give and bestow her unique energies, no such energies will be transferred. The ritual, however elaborately it may be staged, will be an empty one.

Let us therefore close this chapter with a relevant quote from the Brhad Aranyika Upanishad:

> *Her lap is the sacrificial altar,*
> *her hair, the sacrificial grass,*
> *the lips of her Yoni are the fire in the middle . . .*
> *Many mortals . . . go forth from this world . . . without merit,*
> *namely those who practice sexual union without knowing this.*[11]

▼

THE YONI OF FLESH AND BLOOD

*I must practice devotion to women
until I realize the essence of enlightenment.*

CANDAMAHAROSANA TANTRA[1]

Speaking of the Yoni in religious, spiritual, and symbolic terms, as we have so far done throughout this book, one can easily get seduced into regarding the Yoni as a symbol only, as something existing primarily in the lofty regions of the religious mind rather than between the thighs of every woman and goddess. Some modern writers—both Eastern and Western—go far in their attempts to overly abstract and mystify the very real flesh and blood of the Yoni, both as a biological organ of creation and gateway of life and as a potent source of erotic-life energy.

Two such abstract definitions of the Yoni are the "primal root of the source of objectivation" and a "symbol of cosmic mysteries."[2] Such abstract defi-

nitions may sometimes be created in an honest attempt to convey a true sense of religiosity and sacredness regarding a part of the body so often shamefully hidden away. Many times, however, such abstract referencing is merely another shameful denial of the fact that sexuality and fertility were and are part of humanity's most basic and common religious practice.

This chapter is meant to bring us down to earth, to connect us with the physical yoni, taking a close look at the barely recognized and little spoken of variety regarding size, shape, color, texture, feel, and smell that characterizes the yoni.

From the information about rajas revealed in

chapter 6, it should be clear at this point that the yoni is not, as stated in many medical texts, a reproductive system only. The female genitalia are a truly complex and sophisticated system that has as much to do with mutual pleasure as with reproduction, and as much to do with menstrual magic as it does with nourishment of the senses.

YONI VARIETY

Everyone knows that vulvas are far from being all of the same form or appearances.
THE PERFUMED GARDEN[3]

The human mind has a strong tendency toward analyzing and classifying, a tendency that leads us to order our perceptions of the world. Western hermeticist and psychologists have, for example, brought forth the well-known and rather general classifications of humans into psycho-physiological types: choleric, melancholic, phlegmatic, and sanguine. Studies in astrology have rendered twelve archetypes for human nature associated with constellations and planets. In the field of Jungian psychology, women have specifically been typecast into a rather incomplete scheme of mother, amazon, hetaira, and medium.

All these classifications, however, have little insights to offer concerning sexuality and the genitals, and we certainly have no system of describing or classifying the many variations of the yoni itself. One would expect medical texts to deal with this subject in some way, at least in the specialized study of gynecology. However, medical textbooks on the subject of gynecology concern themselves with basic structure only, concentrating on fertility in general and on fungi, bacteria, and disease in particular. Little or nothing can be found that positively discriminates variety in terms of size, shape, texture, color, taste, and smell.

Removed as most of us are from nature and our bodies, many women themselves are unaware of the fact that the yoni is as personal and unique as the face, and that the yoni exists in at least as many obvious varieties as the breasts.▾ (It is a very curious state of affairs that many heterosexual women are less familiar with the visual details of the yoni than are their lovers.) Being more visible in our culture, differences in breast size and shape are universally recognized. However, in some of the Eastern cultures—more supportive of the body and sexuality than the West has ever been—one finds several detailed definitions and classifications not only regarding psycho-physiological typologies of women, but also in regard to the intimate details of the flesh, hair, and juices of the female genitals. Although these descriptions are far from complete and are mainly of male origin, they may perhaps constitute a starting point for a science yet to come.

JAPAN: THE ELEMENTAL YONIS

From Japan we have inherited the following descriptions of five types of female genitals, each associated with one of the five elements: earth, water, fire, air, and ether (or heaven).[4] The classification of the five elemental yonis appeared in a sacred text belonging to the

---

▾ One single bright point of light in this darkness comes from a small but daring publisher in the United States that recently released a book with the beautiful title *Femalia* (see bibliography). The book shows thirty-six different yonis in beautifully reproduced photographs, images not unlike the ones accompanying this chapter. I recommend this work to everyone. It is a balanced portrayal, showing women of different ages and races, and has little text, thus allowing the pictures to speak for themselves. *Femalia* is a welcome and tasteful testimony to the wide variation among women's genitals.

Japanese Tachikawa school entitled *The Sutra of Secret Bliss.*▼ Tachikawa Ryu (see glossary) is an offspring of Shingon Buddhism, one of Japan's largest Buddhist congregations. Both the Shingon and Tachikawa schools have been greatly influenced by Indo-Tibetan Tantra. *The Sutra of Secret Bliss* is now forbidden by religious authorities in Japan.

THE FIVE ELEMENTAL YONIS

1. **Daikoku:** The dark earth yoni, one that envelopes and holds the lingam.

2. **Mizu-tembo:** The moist water yoni, with a small opening and a wide interior.

3. **Ka-tembo:** The hairy fire yoni, ever sweet tasting and insatiable.

4. **Fu-tembo:** The soft wind yoni; also called the Flying Dragon because those who enter this silken tunnel feel as if they are flying in heaven.

5. **Bon-tembo:** The celestial yoni, most beautiful and fragrant; also known as Dragon's Pearl because the tight opening and narrow passage lead to a pearl-like womb, and anyone fortunate enough to enter such a yoni is said to cry out in ecstasy.

CHINA: THE EIGHT VALLEYS AND THE THREE-STORIED TOWER

A prime example of Chinese inquisitiveness is the division of the vaginal tunnel into Eight Valleys (C: *pa-ku*). Here the vagina (about eight centimeters longer than Western medical opinion proposes) is classified into one of eight categories, depending on the depth of the vaginal tunnel. The names of the eight divisions and their corresponding measurements can be found in the Taoist text known as *The Wondrous Discourse of Su Nü*.

THE EIGHT VALLEYS

1. 0–2.5 cm: *ch'in-hsien,* "Zither String" or "Lute String"

2. 5 cm: *ling-ch'ih,* "Water-caltrop Teeth" or "Water-chestnut Teeth"

3. 7.5 cm: *t'o-hsi,* "Peaceful Valley" or "Little Stream"

4. 10 cm: *hsüan-chu,* "Dark Pearl," "Mysterious Pearl"

5. 12.5 cm: *ku-shih,* "Valley Seed" or "Valley Proper"

6. 15 cm: *yü-ch'üeh,* "Palace of Delight" or "Deep Chamber"

7. 17.5 cm: *k'un-hu,* "Inner Door" or "Gate of Posterity"

8. 20 cm: *pei-chi,* "North Pole"

▼ Also known as *The Sutra Proclaiming the Secret Method Enabling a Man and a Woman to Experience the Bliss of Buddhahood in This Very Body.*

Just as the Chinese sexual adepts classified the depths of the vaginal tunnel, they have also studied the relative position of the vulva. Author R. H. van Gulik quotes an ancient Chinese text in which the differences between "high, middle and low vulvae"[5] are discussed, where "high" refers to a forward/upward location and "low" to a place more rearward, closer to the perineum. Whereas in the West it has often been asserted that such differences are racial traits, Chinese and Japanese sources indicate that the location of a woman's vulva is an individual characteristic, and that she and her partner(s) should utilize the advantages of her particular anatomy.

INDIA: THIRTY-SIX COMBINATIONS OF TYPES AND TEMPERAMENTS

In Indian culture we find four "orders," three "temperaments," and three "kinds" of women. Although they speak of only three classes of men, the classical sexological texts of India—mainly the *Kama Sutra,* the *Ananga Ranga,* and the *Koka Shastra*—classify women into thirty-six psycho-physical types. Among the many details pertaining to psycho-physical makeup, most of which are outside the scope of our present topic, this typology also includes descriptions of several types of yonis and the love juices they produce.

THE THREE TEMPERAMENTS

1. The woman of *kapha* (S: "lymphatic") temperament has a yoni that is described as cool and hard, fleshy yet delicate.

2. The woman of *pitta* (S: "bilious") temperament has a yoni that is soft, hot, and relaxed.

3. The woman of *vata* (S: "windy") temperament has a yoni that is not smooth but rough as the tongue of a cow.

THE THREE KINDS

1. The *migri* (S: "female gazelle") or *harini* (S: "doe") is the woman with a deep-set yoni (six fingers deep) that is cool as the moon and has the pleasant scent of a lotus flower.

2. The *vadama* or *ashvini* (S: "mare") is the woman with a yoni nine fingers deep, with freely flowing yellow juices and the scent of sesame.[▼]

3. The *karini* (S: "she-elephant") is the woman with a yoni twelve fingers deep with abundant juices[▼▼] that smell like elephant's musk.

[▼] Alain Daniélou, in his modern translation of the *Kama Sutra* (1994; see bibliography), substitutes "meat" for "sesame."

[▼▼] Here Daniélou substitutes "menses" for juices.

1. The yoni of the *padmini* (S: "lotus woman") is like a flower and enjoys feeling the rays of the sun (to be seen in daylight) and the touch of strong hands. Her love juice is said to smell like a newly blossoming lotus.

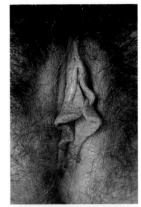

2. The yoni of the *chitrini* (S: "fancy woman") is rounded and soft and easily lubricated, with little pubic hair. Her love juice is said to be exceptionally hot, to smell sweet, and to taste like honey.

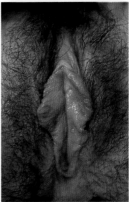

3. The yoni of the *shankhini* (S: the "fairy" or "conch woman") is said to be always moist, to be covered with much hair, and to love being kissed and licked. Her love juice is very abundant and is said to taste salty or acid.

4. The yoni of the *hastini* (S: "elephant woman") is large and deep, and enjoys much stimulation of the clitoris. Her love juice is said to taste and smell like the musky perspiration that collects on a rutting elephant's forehead.

FIGURES 80–83
The four yonis presented here show European women between the age of 35 and 45. Though these yonis may not exactly fit the Indian four orders classification system, they are a good approximation.

The Yoni of Flesh and Blood

ARABIA: ACCEPTANCE OF ENDLESS VARIETY

As indicated by the erotic manual *The Perfumed Garden,* the Arabic culture, with its large collection of names and descriptions for both the yoni (thirty-eight types) and the lingam (thirty-five types), is the most detailed and extensive of all traditions in relationship to the Yoni. While some of the terms and descriptions afford insights into the female psyche and sexual drive, they mostly underscore the truth concerning their (male) origin and orientation. (The author of *The Perfumed Garden,* Sheikh Nefzaoui, seems quite eager to emphasize male virility by speaking often of "entering a hundred times.") However, apart from the criticism such imagery invites from many contemporary people, the Arabic language in regard to the Yoni remains a commendable effort in the way that it so clearly and openly speaks about this most important part of human anatomy, something most people in "liberated" Western societies seem incapable of.

That the following list of terms is not meant merely as a titillating classification for men is evidenced by the fact that throughout *The Perfumed Garden* one finds references to the dream symbology of a particluar yoni type. Dreaming of the yoni of a virgin, for example, means that what one presently desires is yet unattainable. When an open yoni appears in a dream, it signifies that one is fortunate. This text on the erotic arts reads, among other things, as a veritable dream manual.

Here then is a listing of Arabic nomenclature regarding the observed, or sometimes perhaps simply fantasized, varieties of the yoni. (All descriptions are from *The Perfumed Garden.*) Whether one regards these yoni descriptions as ridiculous, pornographic, or perhaps charming, they make one thing quite evident: We are looking here at vestiges of the original awe and magic that has been the province of the yoni ever since time began.

ARABIC DESCRIPTIONS OF THE YONI

El aride (A: "the large one"): The thick and fleshy yoni of a large and heavy woman.

El ass (A: "the primordial"): A general term applied to any kind of yoni.

El cheukk (A: "the chink"): The hard yoni of a very lean or bony woman "with not a vestige of flesh."

El deukkak (A: "the crusher"): A yoni that makes crushing and clinging movements upon the lingam once he has entered, takes him into her grip (with the pelvic muscles) and would, if possible, even absorb a man's testicles. This type of yoni is also known as *el lezzaz* (A: "the unionist"), *el meusass* (A: "the sucker"), *el addad* (A: "the biter").

El feurdj (A: "passage," "opening," "slit"): The most general Arabic term for the yoni, without any typological specifics. The same word is also applied to a passage between two mountains. Interesting is the fact that, with only a slight punctuation mark added, the term means "deliverance from misfortunes."

El gueunfond (A: "the hedgehog"): Name for a yoni "dried up with age and with bristly hair."

El hacene (A: "the beautiful"): A yoni that is white, firm, and plump, "without any deformity" and "vaulted like a dome." A mere look at her makes a "feeble erection into a strong one," and it is almost impossible to take one's eyes off her again.

El harr (A: "the hot one"): The "highly esteemed" yoni that is both tight and warm or even hot, "possessing an intrinsic heat" that equals "the fire of love."

El harrab (A: "the fugitive"): A small and tight yoni that is also "short." With penetration often being painful, she is a "fugitive" trying to evade many types of men.

El hezzaz (A: "the restless"): The eagerly moving yoni of a woman starved for sexual play and enjoyment. Very similar to the descriptions of *el moudd* (A: "the accommodating") and *el mouaine* (A: "the assistant").

El keuss (A: "the vulva"): The name usually used for the "soft, seductive, perfect" and pleasantly smelling yoni of a young woman; "plump and round" in every direction, with long lips, "a grand slit"; dry, yet warm. In the text, the prayer "May God grant us the possession of such a vulva" follows this description.

El laddid (A: "the delicious"): A yoni with "the reputation of affording unprecedented pleasure."

El meusbeul (A: "the long one"): A name for several types of yoni with an outer appearance that is long and reaches from the pubis to the anus. *El meusbeul* seems to lengthen when the woman is standing or lying down yet contracts when she is sitting, "differing in this respect from the vulva of a round shape."

El mokaour (A: "the bottomless"): A deep yoni with a vagina that is longer than usual. Such a woman will require a certain type of partner or activity to truly arouse and satisfy her fully. Similar to *el merour* (A: "the deep one"), which "always has the mouth open."

El neuffakh (A: "the swelling one"): A strange name (or perhaps a bad translation), since the text makes it clear that "swelling" refers not to the yoni but to the male approaching her. The yoni herself is only described as "opening and shutting convulsively," like "the vulva of a mare," at the moment of climax.

El ouasa (A: "the vast one"): A yoni who opens herself widely when excited.

El relmoune (A: "the voluptuous"): A name for the yoni of a young girl or woman before her first coitus.

El sabeur (A: "the resigned"): A yoni that "suffers resignedly" any number of penetrations and even "violent and prolonged coition." Even after "a hundred times," and even with several partners, she would not be annoyed but would rather "give thanks to God."

El sakouti (A: "the silent one"): The yoni who makes no noise, even if she is entered a hundred times.

The Yoni of Flesh and Blood

El taleb (A: "the yearning one"): A name for the yoni of a woman who has been abstinent for too long, or who is naturally more sexually demanding than her partner.

El tseguil (A: "the importunate"): The tireless yoni of a free and passionate woman with strong sexual demands who "would want still more" even after a hundred times. Typically fearful of such women, who are the "pursuer" instead of the "pursued," the author writes: "Luckily, it is a rarity, and only found in a small number of women who are wild with passion, all on fire, aglow." Little did he know ….

El zerzour (A: "the starling"): The yoni of a very young girl.

El zeunbour (A: "the wasp"): A yoni receiving her name by the nature of the pubic hair surrounding it, or as the text describes it, by "the strength and roughness of its fur." To the entering lingam the hair feels like stings from a wasp.

Last but not least, *The Perfumed Garden* provides us with a number of names that seem to concentrate not so much on the yoni as a whole as on the specific appearance of the clitoris or the labia.

Abou cheuffrine (A: "the double-lipped"): A yoni with lips that are either "long and hanging" or that are exceptionally thick and large, as in the case of some very full women.

Abou djebaha (A: "one with a projection"): A name for a large yoni "with a projecting, fleshy forehead."

Abou khochime (A: "the snub nose"): Name for a yoni with "thin lips" and a small "tongue" (small clitoris).▾

Abou tertour (A: "the crested one"): A yoni with a "red comb, like that of a cock, which rises at the moment of enjoyment."

Medical science, biology, and psychology attempt to know every minute variety of human nature and the mind, but these disciplines fail completely when it comes to human sexuality. As already stated, within the realm of biology and medicine one studies the yoni and the womb in terms of fertility and diseases only; within sexology one studies measurements, contractions, dilations, and orgasms. If we as a culture allow ourselves to put aside the Judeo-Christian shame connected to the sexual aspects of the body and embrace the Eastern acceptance of yoni variety, we can develop a comparative aesthetics that would make every woman appreciate her uniqueness.

▼

▾ In China, the clitoris is often named the "golden tongue."

CONTEMPORARY CULTURE AND THE YONI

Drawing and masturbating were the first sacred experiences I remember. Both activities began when I was about 4 years old. Exquisite sensations produced in my body and images that I made on paper tangled with language, religion, everything I was taught. As a result I thought that the genital was where God lived.

ARTIST CAROLEE SCHNEEMAN[1]

After all that we have read and seen so far in this book, Carolee Schneeman's memory of her childhood experiences should come as no surprise. That a young girl would associate spiritual, sacred, or religious feelings with the concept of God rather than Goddess is emblematic of our modern society. Once this particular girl had grown up to be an artist, well informed about the female role in ancient religions and cultures, she understood the symbolism contained in her childhood thoughts and feelings all too clearly. Since the time of her own coming of age, the time when she reached this realization, most of Carolee's works have been dedicated to the Goddess or her priestesses.

Unfortunately, such a realization has not yet been attained by many in our so-called enlightened and liberated culture. As we will see in this chapter, most people never get beyond the most simple and often ignorant level of regard for women or the Yoni.

Language reflects the sorry state of our cultural concepts, and this is especially true in the context of terminology used for the Yoni. However, the same dearth of appropriate language also permeates the world of erotic or sexual art. With few exceptions, most erotic novels and books on erotic art will not describe the Yoni as a beautiful flower or as a source of power; they will instead use derogatory or neutral terms, or show the Yoni (and women) as defiled or dangerous or as mere objects of lust.

There are exceptions, however, in the realms of

both language and art. In the following section the reader will find several positive and respectful terms. Although they originated in cultures other than ours, some of them can nevertheless be used with grace. Indeed, the term *yoni* itself has lately begun enjoying more widespread use, not only in private circles but also on the Internet. A similar tendency toward respectful depiction of the Yoni can be noticed in the visual arts. As this chapter shows, more artists are daring to illustrate the Yoni as a beautiful part of the female body. Other women go so far as to make the Yoni itself into a work of art by adorning and ornamenting their inner and outer lips with jewelry or tattoos. By thus returning to an ancient custom followed by many tribal peoples, these modern body artists reiterate the respect for the Yoni held by the ancients.

YONI TERMINOLOGY

Everywhere the world over, people have invented words and phrases for the genitals. Such words were sometimes those of honest, sheer delight regarding the organs of pleasure and can be recognized as terms of endearment meant for friends and the beloved. Other words were clearly meant to remain more or less secret within a certain group, and thereby constituted a kind of code. However, those societies—one can hardly call them "cultures"—where sexual pleasures were or are strongly repressed, inhibited, deplored, or outlawed, most often develop a genital terminology that is mainly vulgar, expressing fear rather than awe and focusing on the scatological rather than the delightful.

Such societies have always had their deviant members, those who do not share the generally negative sentiments and who know the psychological, spiritual, and health-promoting forces of eros and sexuality. Such people, often labeled heretics or hedonists invented their own languages for acts and aspects of physical love. In Tantra, Taoism, and alchemy, such terms were often consciously designed to go unrecognized by outsiders, evolving from a need for secrecy in times when sexual experimentation, whether sacred or profane, was not socially accepted or encouraged. Often such a secret language consisted of everyday words that had simple and familiar exoteric meanings as well as hidden meanings. Such words were often either drawn from nature, and included names of fruits, plants, and animals, or derived from humanity's inventions in the sphere of agriculture and industry, as indicated by such names as plow or hammer (male) and chimney or anvil (female).

On the following pages we will look at a variety of terms peoples of various ages and cultures have used to describe the Yoni. The terms have been grouped here according to their inherent meanings. (I leave the task of subdividing these words into categories such as "derogatory," "slang," "artful," "colloquial," "medical," "euphemistic," "romantic," or "respectful" to each reader and her or his sensibilities.) Reading through this list once again makes it evident how very male oriented and blatantly sexist is our language when it comes to matters of sexuality. However, the roots of this evil are not to be found in men alone, or in their centuries-old perception of women as possessions or the mere objects of lust. When one looks at a similar list of terms for the phallus it becomes clear that the existing terminology is, with few exceptions, equally disrespectful and lacking in both sensitivity and appreciation. I must therefore draw the conclusion that the major underlying cause for this state of affairs is to be found in all sexually repressive religions and the cultures and societies they have spawned.

If a society is to transform its thinking about sexuality, it must also change its language. On the most fundamental level, it is up to fathers and mothers, and perhaps teachers as well, to stop associating sexuality with shame and to rather instill their daughters, sons, and students with a sense of healthy regard for all aspects of the physical body. Perhaps after carefully studying this list, some readers may feel motivated to change their own habits of speaking and thinking.

THE MANY NAMES OF THE YONI

* Terms based on the Greek *konnos* and the subsequent Latin *cunnus* were derived from the names of the goddesses known as Kunthus, a Greek goddess of fertility, and Kunti, an Indian goddess of nature and earth. Such terms include *con, conch, concha, conno, coño, count, cunt, cunte, kunthus, kunti,* and *kut.*

* Terms based on the general shape, color, and texture of the yoni, including some traditional yoni symbols, include *artichoke, cabbage, cinnabar cleft, cinnabar gate, conch, concha, daisy, eye, fig, ivory gate, kteis* (scallop), *lily, long eye, lotus, nether eye, nether mouth, O, oyster, padma* (lotus), *papaya, plum, rose, split apricot,* and *velvet sheath.*

* Terms indicating a specific shape, size, or position of the yoni include *cave* (large yoni), *chu-bin, ge-bin,* and *jo-bin.*

- Terms indicating the taste and/or smell of the yoni include *civet, fish, living fountain,* and *pillow of musk.*

- Terms for the yoni in connection with the surrounding pubic hair and/or the pubic mound include *ace* (from *ace of spades,* meaning "pubic hair"), *beaver, bunny, cat, chat* (French for cat), *coyote, crown and feathers, cushion, downy bit, fleece, green grove, green meadow, moss rose, muff, pussy,* and *squirrel.*

- Terms representing the yoni in terms of fertility or motherhood include *alembic, cwithe* (also *kvithe, queynthe,* or *quaint*), *doorway of life, fish, fruitful vine, ka-t, living fountain, nursery, orchard,* and *retort.*

- Terms representing the yoni as an opening, entrance, or passage include *alley, black hole, bottomless pit, chimney, cinnabar cleft, cinnabar hole, crevice, Cupid's alley, dark gate, dead-end street, golden gate, heavenly gate, happy valley, hole of holes, ivory gate, jade door, jade gate, main avenue, marble arch, mysterious gate, mysterious valley, orifice, slit, tunnel, twat,* and *vent.*

- Terms representing the yoni as a container or dwelling include *alembic, box, cave, cellar, chalice, cylinder, den, golden gully, grotto, gully, home sweet home, precious crucible, retort, secret cavern, sensitive cave,* and *trinket.*

- Terms indicating sexual attraction, delight, and respect include *center of attraction, center of bliss, center of desire, happy valley, heaven, heavenly gate, inner heart, lotus of her wisdom, Mount Pleasant, mystic rose, paradise, pleasure garden, precious crucible, promised land, pure lily, sensitive cave, shrine of love,* and *treasury.*

- Terms representing the yoni as something tasty and edible, based on the wide-spread practice (or fantasy) of cunnilingus, include *bread, bun, cake, cookies, jam, jelly-roll, muffin, orange, oyster, papaya, plum,* and *tidbit.*

- Terms based partly on the boyish (and ignorant) Freudian perception of the yoni as a wound—that is, as missing a lingam—and partly on observations such as menstrual bleeding, include *chink, cleft, crack, cranny, crease, crevice, cut, furrow, gash, quiff or quim* (cleft), *slit, split, sulcus* (furrow), and *wound.*

- Terms representing the yoni as something dark, shameful, and to be hidden include *black hole, dark gate, hidden place, ludibria, pit of darkness, pudendum,* and *tunnel.*

- Terms based on male fears include *black hole, bottomless pit, carnal trap, dead-end street, hell, man-trap, noose, pit of darkness, snatch,* and *vagina dentata.*

- Terms defining the yoni in complementary relationship with the lingam (given in brackets) include *ghanta* (vajra), *honeypot* (honey=semen), *lock* (key), *magnet* (pole), and *mortar* (pestle).

- Terms for specific parts of the yoni, such as labia (l), clitoris (c), or vagina (v), include *alley* (v), *bell* (l), *boy in the boat* (c), *carnal trap* (v), *cookies* (l), *cunnicle / cunnikin* (v), *Cupid's alley* (v), *ditch* (v), *drain* (v), *eye* (v), *fish pond* (v), *flap* (l), *garden gate* (v), *gate of jewels* (v), *hot lips* (l), *nether lips* (l), *pit of darkness* (v), *sugar basin* (v), *taste bud* (c), *tunnel* (v), and *two-leafed book* (l).

The terms listed here are shown alphabetically in appendix II. The appendix listing also gives a brief etymology, when known.

MODERN ARTISTS AND ANCIENT MYTHS

After reading the previous chapters that dealt mainly with cultures and religions of days gone by, many readers will likely feel that worship of the Yoni, worship in the sense of true and living *religio* (L: "connection to sacredness"), is sorely lacking in today's spiritual landscape.

In one sense, this is true, at least as long as we look for it only at the level of actual practice. If, however, we look for evidence of Yoni worship in other areas, traces of the old or the beginnings of something new can be found. A look at various aspects of modern-day society shows clearly that the veneration of the Yoni has simply undergone a transformation. It is a process quite similar to the one we have seen in Japan, where the modern tokudashi displays key elements from the ancient Kagura ritual (see chapter 5). When we dare to look for evidence of Yoni worship we can see that the most ancient and most fundamentally human religion has simply taken other forms in order to survive in present-day culture. Although in art and literature sexual desire most often underlies depictions or personifications of the Yoni, there are also many examples of illustrations and descriptions that bear witness to a continued worship.

For example, the following verses, spawned in the rock-and-roll subculture of the 1960s and 1970s, are an unmistakable reiteration of the ancient wisdom described in the first chapters of this book.

You know, when you're born,
you first see light of day
through the gap between your mother's legs,
… that's the truth…

and from that minute on, most of us guys,
and some of you girls,
spend our life trying to get into a hole
… hhmmm…

But don't worry,
because if you make it, if you don't make it,
they gonna dig a hole for you eventually in the ground,
and slut you right back to Mother Earth…

Mother Earth is waiting for you, yes she is…

ERIC BURDON[2]

We can find ample evidence of modern Yoni worship within the cultural landscape that is continually formed and re-formed by the media. For example, over the last decade the media have picked up on the noticeable revival of Goddess worship, present in the form of Wicca and other religious groups and personalities who orient themselves toward nature, Earth, and the Goddess, and as such often toward the Yoni as well. The ever-growing number of books, magazine articles, and lectures/workshops focused on this revival is bringing Goddess worship closer to mainstream consciousness.

A variety of artists seem to be outspoken modern-day Yoni worshippers. Such artists range from Gustave Courbet (1819–77), Georgia O'Keeffe (1887–1986), and Andre Masson (1896–1987) to Judy Chicago (b. 1939), Eric Burdon (b. 1941), Christina Camphausen (b. 1953), and Vincent Dame (1946–1995). However, regardless of appearances, each of these artists have (had) personal motivations for making his or her art. Georgia O'Keeffe, for example, distanced herself from anyone, such as Anais Nin (1903–1977) and others of her contemporaries, who recognized the female genitals in her work. At the time, those in literary, art, and other learned circles were recently exposed to the new teachings of Sigmund Freud (1865–1939). To those such as Nin who found Yoni imagery in her art, O'Keeffe would reply that what they saw originated from their own sexual obsessions.

A passage from Nin's *Delta of Venus* alludes to her vision of O'Keeffe's work. In the passage, several men are discussing sexuality in art; one of them makes the following statement:

> "They're not flowers," said the pipe-smoker, "they're vulvas. Anyone can see that. At first it looks like petals, the heart of a flower, then one sees the two uneven lips, the fine center line, the wavelike edge of the lips when they are spread open.[3]

FIGURE 86
In this work, artist Judy Chicago clearly shows that she's explored the worldwide myths concerning the worship of the Goddess and the Yoni. The painting's title, The Cunt as Temple, Tomb, Cave or Flower, *aptly condenses most of the information presented in this book.*

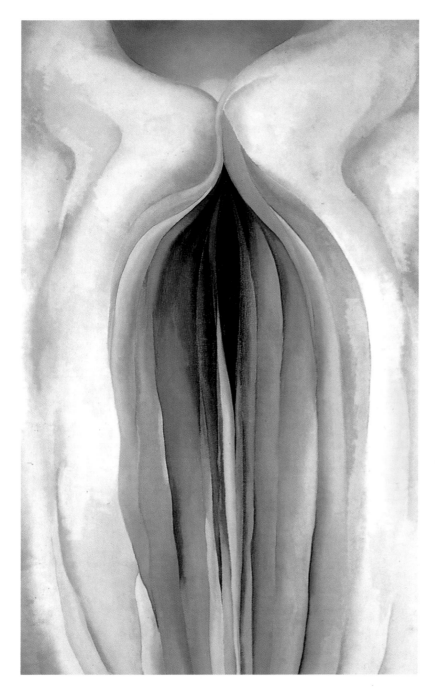

It is no coincidence that the same quote has been used to describe the work of artist Christina Camphausen.[4] The major difference between her work and that of O'Keeffe, however, is that Camphausen's drawings are not flowers that look like Yonis; they are rather Yonis that resemble beautiful flowers. Although some of Camphausen's work is slightly symbolic (see pages v, viii, and 66), most of her pieces are intended to show the great beauty and variety of female genitalia and to raise people's awareness of this through her artwork.

A unique and stunning approach to our subject is that of Judy Chicago, who makes distinct connections between her reverence for women, the religions of the Goddess, and artistic depiction of the Yoni. In her monumental sculpture *The Dinner Party*, Chicago honored thirty-nine important women of the past and present by creating a dinner table set with an elaborately painted china plate and an embroidered runner for each woman. Chicago thus created a virtual dinner party celebrating female achievement through history. Each of the plates features a Yoni, some symbolically abstract and others quite lifelike.[5]

Whereas fewer people today are shocked or outraged about explicitly sexual or genital depictions in art, only a decade ago and for centuries preceding that, public and private censorship of sexual art was the norm. Gustave Courbet's beautiful painting *Origin of the World* was stored in a chest, the painting kept secret so as not to put the artist's reputation at stake. His Irish model, Joanne Hiffernan, was, for her time, just as daring as the painter who became famous (posthumously) for his highly realistic nudes. In an equally controversial work of the same year,[▼] the same model is shown in a scene of two women making love. *Origin of the World* seemed for all intents and purposes to have disappeared from the face of the earth; although a photographic reproduction existed, the original was believed to have been destroyed. In 1995 the piece was found in the collection of the late Jaques Lacan and was permanently placed in the Courbet room of the Musée d'Orsay in Paris. In naming his open-legged nude *Origin of the World*, Courbet catapulted this work into a sphere beyond the purely sexual or pornographic and into the realm of myth.

The question whether Courbet consciously named his piece in relationship to his awareness of the stories and practices of ancient peoples is one we cannot answer. In

▼ Courbet, 1866: *The Two Friends.*

FIGURE 89
An example from Judy Chicago's monumental work The Dinner Party, *a grand celebration of womanity. On a large triangular table, dinner plates were set out for 39 important women of the past and present; this plate is for celebrated author Virginia Woolf (1882–1941).*

FIGURE 90
For his time, Gustave Courbet's Origin of the World *(1866) was a daringly realistic and explicit work of art. Although his title suggests a respectful stance towards the Yoni, his contemporaries could not but regard this as pornography.*

FIGURE 91 (OPPOSITE ABOVE)
The installation Surrounded Islands *(1983) in the Biscayne Bay of Greater Miami, Florida, by artists Christo and Jeanne Claude.*

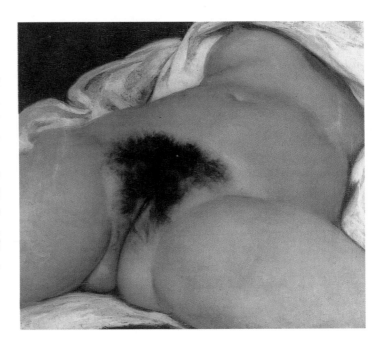

today's world, one in which a global media network provides us with the most diverse information about near and far-away cultures—including access to indigenous myths, legends, and practices—it is difficult to ascertain whether an artist creates something purely from her or his inner vision, or whether the outward expression has been directly influenced by something she or he heard, saw, or read. Thus, when I see Christo's *Surrounded Islands* it brings to my mind the legendary Yoni-shaped island of Jambu, the Indian version of paradise. If Christo had heard of Jambu, it is possible that *Surrounded Islands* is his visual interpretation of that legend. In that case his rendering of the island would indicate his regard for the Yoni. If, on the other hand, Christo had not been previously aware of this legendary place, his painting shows once again that archetypal images surface across cultures and time.

With the work of many other artists, this question simply does not arise. Either the work itself or the title given it by the artist clearly reveals that it was inspired by ancient myths and legends concerning the Yoni or, in some cases, by existent original works that were discovered by archeological research or through traveling. Examples of artists who are decidedly aware of these spiritual and mythological roots are Carolee Schneeman, Ana Mendieta, Christina Camphausen, Clara Meneres, Judy Chicago, Niki de Saint Phalle, and Vincent Dame, to name but a few whose work is shown in this book.

FIGURE 92
In 1966, artist Niki de Saint Phalle created the huge hollow sculpture The Figure Hon, *daring visitors to walk between a woman's open legs into her Yoni.*

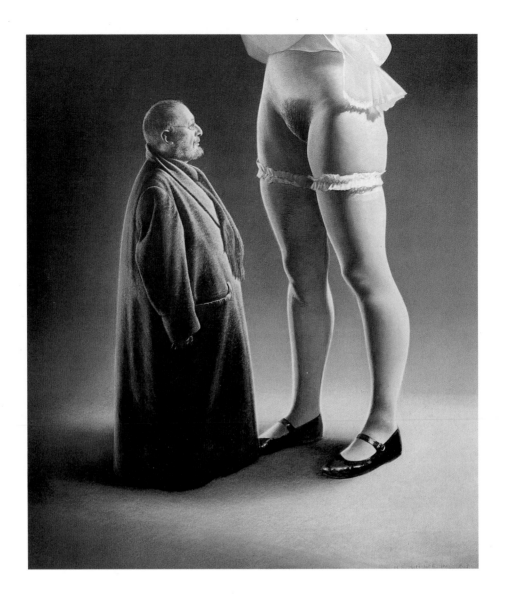

FIGURE 93
Fascination as well as a feeling of
inferiority are depicted in artist
Gottfried Helnwein's surreal
work Lulu *(1988), an imagery*
harking back to prehistoric
times.

Another group of artists approaches the subject of the Yoni from an entirely different point of view. Some, such as Gottfried Helnwein in his *Lulu* or Andre Masson in *Erotic Earth*, seem to externalize inner visions that belong to the realm of modern psychoanalysis; others, such as Denish, approach our subject from the more religiously motivated and spiritually oriented stance of a contemporary worshiper.

However different the mindset of various artists may be, their imagery—being so central and truly archetypal to humanity—is often quite similar in tone. For example, does not the poem opposite, written by Denish, then a practitioner of Indian Tantra, read like an interpretation of a Freudian fantasy from the subconscious of an artist such as Masson?

Although contemporary and of non-Indian origin, this poem represents true Tantric art, a qualification that one could perhaps also apply to the sculpture *Cosmic Egg* (figure 95, page 94) by Dutch artist Vincent Dame. The question "What is Tantric art?" has become a widely discussed topic in Indian art, gallery, and art magazine circles. The general opinion seems to be that true Tantric art can be created only by someone who actually

noisiv ənivib rəd

looking beyond
those well formed
roundish fleshy hills
of duality

through
that gorgeous flat land
of her lower grounds

right over
that triangled forestlike
somewhat bushy area

one beholds
the mother goddess

images
of her smiling face
soft and juicy lips
shining rims
on a golden chalice
filled to the brim
with that divine nectar

her great bliss
ever available
to those ones
who dare to drink
and drown
in ecstasy[6]

her divine vision

looking beyond
those well formed
roundish fleshy hills
of duality

through
that gorgeous flat land
of her lower grounds

right over
that triangled forestlike
somewhat bushy area

one beholds
the mother goddess

images
of her smiling face
soft and juicy lips
shining rims
on a golden chalice
filled to the brim
with that divine nectar

her great bliss
ever available
to those ones
who dare to drink
and drown
in ecstasy[6]

FIGURE 94 (ABOVE)
Erotic Earth by French
surrealist Andre Masson is
another example of man's
desire to get back into where
he came from.

The mirror image of his poem
"her divine vision" (left)
reveals the Yoni about which
Denish writes.

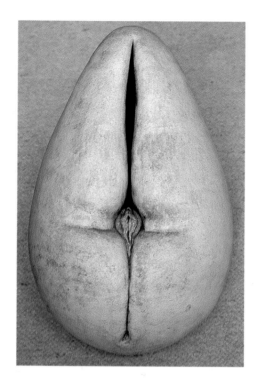

practices Tantra. Tantric art, in fact, is not made for the marketplace but is instead a mode of practice, yet another form of personal worship. It is not enough for an artist to incorporate a triangle or a lotus or a goddess figure into his or her work and call it Tantric art. Although contemporary fashion and Western interests might encourage artists and galleries to sell such images as Tantric art, they are not authentic. True Tantric art comes into existence by means of personal vision and dedication combined with traditional knowledge and true initiation.

Such a combination of vision and knowledge can be found in literature as well. The novels of Jean M. Auel are an outstanding example of fiction that simultaneously incorporates a detailed knowledge of history and archeology. The widespread worship of the Goddess in Old Europe during the Stone Age is the backdrop for the series that began with *The Clan of the Cave Bear.* In her books Auel also includes details about ritual defloration, sacred prostitution, the ritual use of psychotropic substances, and the revolutionizing act of an artisan carving the first portrayal of a living person's body and face. Although Auel's novels do not describe Yoni worship per se, they are stimulating and educational to read simply because they allow us to imagine and visualize—with the help and guidance of a skilled writer—the lives and lifestyles, the hopes, fears, and religious visions of our ancestors. Several other authors, including Joan Grant, Philip José Farmer, Morgan Llywelyn, and Abraham Merritt, have also written fiction works inspired by matriarchal and Goddess-oriented cultures (see bibliography).

YONI ADORNMENT

The very same decades that, through electronics and multimedia venues, have ushered humanity into the age of the digital primate have also seen the revival of an ancient practice—that of fashioning the human body into a living work of art. Just as many modern women pierce their ears in order to wear beautiful ear adornments, tribal women pierced or tattooed their inner or outer labia or their clitoris for pleasure and beauty. After hundreds or thousands of years, many women are once again discovering the empowerment and pleasure that can accompany adornment of the Yoni. Body modification in general and Yoni adornment in particular, once reserved to the underground movements of most "cultured" societies, has now gone mainstream. Your neighbor may be pierced or your coworker may have a tattoo, even if you have never seen it or heard about it.

In India and among many tribal peoples of Oceania, tattooing the Yoni has been a rather common practice and was duly reported—sometimes with horror and sometimes with amazement—by the early travelers and missionaries to those regions. Given our cultural indoctrination, many people shy away not only from such practices but also from their known practitioners. However, if one takes the time to read some of the literature now available,[7] it becomes clear that genital piercing and the piercing of one's nipples is not done merely for the added sexual stimulation it affords oneself and others. People often undertake such endeavors with a true sense of spirituality, initiation, or personal freedom, concepts rarely associated with such practices by those who value "normality" above individuality.

Pain and blood—the two experiences most of us associate with piercing, and two experiences most of us have been trained to abhor and fear—are of little concern to those who take the steps necessary to turn some part of the body into a personalized work of art. Both those who give and those who receive tattoos and piercings often speak of feeling primitive during the experience; some speak of finally feeling connected to others, feeling part of a tribe or family.

Piercing or tattooing the body, and especially such sensitive and private parts of the body, may not be for everyone. Although it was widely done by our ancient ancestors and is being practiced again today on a larger scale than most people imagine, no one has to or should be made to do it; you should either do it only for yourself or not do it at all.

I want to stress the importance of respecting others' choices in all respects, but especially in regard to the body and to spiritual and sexual expressions, preferences, and practices. Whether someone worships the Yoni, the Lingam, or a seminude man dying on a cross is irrelevant. Diversity of expression is our human heritage, and it will always be that way. When all of us are well informed about the hows and whys of the actions and choices people make, and when we not only tolerate but respect those choices, the world will be a more humane and subsequently less painful place in which to live. In my view the best effort we could make toward a less repressed and less aggressive world would be for people everywhere to throw off the burden of the Judeo-Christian teachings and make positive contact with their bodies and with the place from which we all come: the Origin of the World and the Source of All—the Yoni, and Woman.

FIGURE 96
Body adornment. In essence, piercing one's genitals is not truly different from piercing one's earlobe. It does, however, require a positive view of the body and sexuality.

Yoni Topography: The Female Genital System

A work of multiple volumes is needed to describe in all its biological and medical detail something so miraculously complex as the female genital system. Some such works do, in fact, exist,[1] and I would encourage you to consult those for a most thorough presentation on the topic. However, a book dedicated to the yoni cannot forego this topic entirely. I therefore present here the most basic information on the female genital system. It is my experience that, while rudimentary, such a sketch tends to raise awareness and knowledge, given that most of us have been deprived of the motivation to even *want* to know about "femalia." Please note that the descriptions given here are general in nature; in testimony to the unique presentations of nature, tremendous variations exist among all women. The numbers that appear in the text correspond to those used in figure 97 opposite.

1 PUBIS

The triangle of hair that covers the mons veneris (2) and much of the labia majora (3). This area also contains scent glands.

In China, female pubic hair is generally known as *yinmao;* other poetic Chinese phrases include "black rose," "fragrant grass," "sacred hair," or "moss." Women without any pubic hair are known as "white tigers." To the Chinese, an equilateral triangle with an upward directed growth is a sign of beauty, and abundant hair is regarded as a sign of sensuality and passion. The existence of such phrases in the Chinese language suggests that they are able to talk about the female sexual organs more freely than we do.

2 MONS VENERIS

The "mount of Venus" or mons pubis refers to the cushion of fatty tissue that protects the pubic bones and that separates to become the labia majora (3).

A Chinese name for the female mons is "hill of sedge."

3 LABIA MAJORA
(L: *labium majus,*
sing.)

The large or outer lips of the vagina, extending from the mons veneris (2) to the perineum (22). The labia majora contain sebaceous (oil secreting) scent glands and a small number of sweat glands. After puberty, the pigmented outer skin of the labia majora begins to grow pubic hair, while the insides remain smooth and hairless. Like the labia minora (4), the labia majora often swell during sexual arousal. The two clitoral bulbs of spongy, erectile tissue responsible for the lips swelling during arousal lie between the labia majora and the forks of the clitoris (11). Another term used for these beautiful lips is "lips of the myrtle," so called by the first-century Greek physician Rufus of Ephesus.

4 LABIA MINORA
(L: *labium minus,*
sing.)

These small or inner lips of smooth, hairless skin, mostly hidden by the labia majora (3), are generally colored in various shades of pink. The labia minora contain sweat glands and sebaceous scent glands that are instrumental in their moistening. During sexual arousal the labia minora can become engorged with blood and swell to two or three

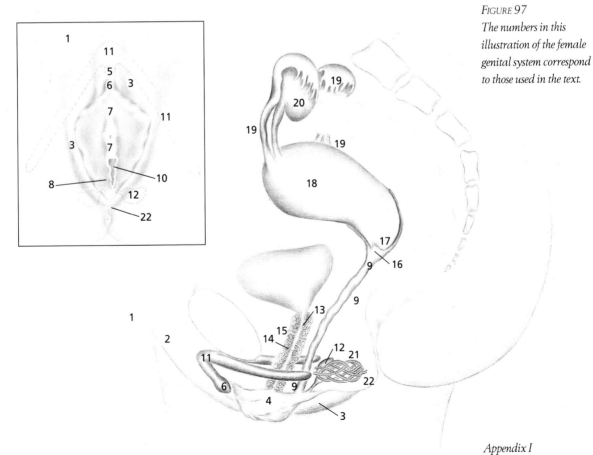

FIGURE 97
The numbers in this illustration of the female genital system correspond to those used in the text.

times their usual size, often undergoing changes in color as well. At their upper end, the labia minora join to form the clitoral hood (5). The small fold connecting the labia minora to the vaginal opening is known as the *fourchette* (French).

These sensitive lips are sometimes called *nymphae* (Greek); it is interesting to note that before it was used to describe the woman's inner lips this word meant "water goddesses." The word *nymphae* was first used by Rufus of Ephesus (first-century Greece) to describe "the little piece of flesh in its [the cleft's] middle."[2] In choosing this expression, Rufus of Ephesus seems to have recognized that women are capable of ejaculating. Rufus also coined the expression "fruit of the myrtle" for the labia minora.

In the Chinese language, the labia minora are known as "red pearls" (C: *ch'ih-chu*) or "wheat buds," their lower meeting point as "jade veins" (C: *yü-li*), and the point near the clitoral crown (6) as "lute strings."

5 CLITORAL HOOD

A small, freely moveable fold of skin formed by the joining of the labia minora (4). It completely covers the shaft of the clitoris (11) and forms a protective hood that wholly or partially covers the clitoral crown (6). In China, the hood was known as "dark garden," "god field," and "grain seed."

6 CLITORAL CROWN
(Lowndes crown, glans clitoridis)

The relatively small, visible part of the clitoris is what most people think of as the entire clitoris (11). This crown, so named by Josephine Lowndes-Sevely (see bibliography), consists of tissue known as the *corpus spongiosum* (see glossary) that contains a large number of nerve endings, thus rendering it one of the most highly sensitive aspects of the female anatomy. During sexual arousal the clitoral crown can change color and increase in size, often projecting itself far out of the clitoral hood (5). It is the clitoral crown (not the whole clitoris, as is sometimes reported) that is cut away in those unfortunate girls who undergo clitoridectomy.

Just below the crown, where the labia minora (4) appear to meet, is another highly sensitive area known as the frenulum of the clitoris, or in China as "lute strings." To the Tachikawa adepts of Japan (see glossary), the most appropriate name for the clitoris was *hoju*, a term that in Buddhism also signifies the "magic jewel of the dharma."

7 VAGINAL GLANS What Josephine Lowndes-Sevely has simply named the "woman's glans" is the small area of skin below the clitoral crown (6) and above the opening to the vagina (9), including the meatus of the urethra (13). Like the clitoral crown, this female glans is a highly sensitive zone with a great number of nerve endings. The glans is very flexible and, during sexual union, moves in and out of the vagina, creating a pleasurable sensation for the woman."[3]

8 VESTIBULE This outer room or entrance chamber to the vagina (9) is surrounded and enclosed by the labia minora (4). The vestibule contains the openings to the urethra (13), the vagina, and the two ducts coming from the vulvovaginal glands (12) and receives secretions from all those as well. The vestibule also contains the vaginal glans (7), two elongated bodies of erectile tissue, and many mucus-secreting glands.

Chinese terms for this vaginal entrance are "heavenly court" (C: *t'ien-t'ing*), "secluded valley" (C: *yu-ku*), and "examination hall."

9 VAGINA A deeply folded muscular tube connecting the vestibule (8) to the cervix (17). The healthy vagina is capable of great distention and is highly lubricated by its mucous membranes. In concert with the vaginal muscles, it plays a most important role in sexual union, a role often neglected in medical textbooks. The vagina is the pathway traveled by menstrual fluids, by sperm cells on their way to the ovum, and by the birthing baby. The vaginas of most women also contain odorous aliphatic acids, responsible for each woman's distinctive vaginal scent. A Japanese expression for the vagina is "gate of jewels." In matters of sexual anatomy, Oriental cultures are generally much more respectful than Western ones, reminding us that they studied sexuality as both an art and a science.

The term *vagina* is often used when one is actually referring to the yoni-vulva as a whole.

10 HYMEN The opening to the vagina (9) is covered by a membranous fold of skin known as the hymen. After defloration, fragments of the hymen will often remain as part of the vaginal opening.

English use of the term *hymen* dates back to the seventeenth century; the word was most likely derived from the name of a Greco-Roman god of marriage, also named Hymen.[4]

The widely accepted notion that all women are born with a hymen that breaks and bleeds when contacted with pressure is refuted by medical statistics indicating that only 42 percent of all women are born with a "normal" hymen, whereas in 47 percent of all women the hymen is highly flexible, and in 11 percent it is so thin that it will break easily and at an early age through nonsexual body movement.[5]

11 CLITORIS

Generally regarded solely as part of the female anatomy, it has now become clear that men also have a clitoris.[▼] In both woman and man, the clitoral shaft and the two *crura* ("legs") of the clitoris consist of a tissue called the *corpus cavernosum* (L: "body of caves"; see glossary). In women, the clitoris is a relatively large structure of erectile tissue, most of which is inside the body and hidden from view. Apart from the glans or crown (6), the clitoris consists of a shaft and the forked crura. Each crura runs downward and inward below the clitoral bulbs at their respective sides of the labia majora (3). Like its visible crown, the shaft or *corpus* of the clitoris becomes erect and enlarged by the increased blood pressure that occurs during sexual stimulation. The highly sensitive shaft usually moves involuntarily when touched.

Other words for the female clitoris are the Chinese "golden tongue," "seat of pleasure," "golden terrace," or "jade terrace," the Latin *naviculus* ("little boat"), the Sanskrit *madanahatra,* and the contemporary lesbian slang expression "boy in the boat." If the Chinese seem eloquent in their erotic language, it might be interesting to know that the Maori of New Zealand are known to have more words for the clitoris than any other people anywhere.

12 VULVOVAGINAL GLANDS
(Bartholin's glands, vestibular glands)

These two tiny glands are located to the left and right of the vagina (9), between the vaginal wall and the lower labia minora (4). The vulvovaginal glands secrete a thick protein compound via the two Bartholin's ducts into the vestibule (8). The major purpose of these glands, apart from lubrication of the vaginal opening, seems to be the generation of a stimulating sexual odor. As such they may be related to the estrous cycle, the scent glands, and pheromone attraction.

The Chinese have several terms for these glands,

[▼] For anyone still believing in the Freudian notion of penis envy, the realization that the penis is simply the male manifestation of the clitoris—or that both, in fact, are of the same embryological origin—should be illuminating. For details on this, see Lowndes Sevely, *Eve's Secrets.*

including "infant girl," "mixed rock," and "sun terrace." The Sanskrit *purnacandra* (S: "full moon"), defined in the *Koka Shastra* as a duct or channel within the yoni and said to be filled with the "juice of love," probably refers to the ducts of these vulvovaginal glands.

13 URETHRA

In both women and men, the urethra is a tube that transports urine from the bladder toward its external opening, the meatus of the vaginal glans (7) of woman and the glans penis of man. A woman's urethra is approximately four centimeters long and is surrounded by the urethral sponge (14).

14 URETHRAL SPONGE

The urethral sponge is a sheath of tissue (corpus spongiosum) surrounding the female urethra (13). It consists of a number of glands, ducts, blood vessels, and fleshy tissue, including the paraurethral glands and ducts, a term that is now commonly replaced by *female prostatic glands* (15) (see below). One part of the urethral sponge in particular has been proposed as a vital element of the female genital system; for many women, its stimulation can be instrumental in reaching orgasm and/or discharging orgasmic fluids. This widely publicized part of the urethral sponge is known as the G-spot. The G-spot is said to be a sensitive area internal to the vagina, about halfway between the mons veneris (2) and the cervix (17). For a more detailed discussion of the G-spot, see the glossary.

15 PROSTATIC GLANDS (female)

Embedded in the urethral sponge (14) are a number of prostatic glands, similar in makeup and function to those of the male. Only recently discovered as such,[6] they were hitherto known as paraurethral glands. The prostatic glands are connected by a large number of ducts to the female urethra (13); these ducts transport the glandular liquids. Although the glands' specific functions are as yet unknown, they likely constitute the actual erotogenic pressure point known as the G-spot. Their liquids are one element of the female love juices that make female ejaculation a reality to be denied only by the most die-hard chauvinists.

16 OS

This tiny opening at the tip of the cervix (17) is sometimes called the mouth of the uterus (18). The os provides a passageway from the vagina (outer os) into the uterus (inner os) and vice versa, yet cannot be penetrated by either finger or lingam. After enlargement, which occurs during childbirth, it closes tightly again.

17 CERVIX

The cervix constitutes the lower part or neck of the uterus (18). It projects forward into the vagina (9) and can often be felt there by a probing finger, depending on the woman's position.

18 UTERUS

The uterus, which includes the os (16) and the cervix (17), is a pear-shaped, hollow, muscular organ. Its usual size is that of a small avocado pear, yet dimension, as well as orientation within the pelvis, changes with position and sexual excitation. The inner lining of the uterus, known as the endometrium, undergoes several changes throughout the menstrual/ovarian cycle.

The uterus is the actual womb within which all humans develop. The birthing infant leaves this dark, warm, aquatic environment via cervix (17), os (16), and vagina (9) for the world outside. The alchemist's alembic (see page 33) has been fashioned to resemble the uterus; the term is thus often used as a code word when referring to the yoni.

The Taoists have called the uterus by such secret names as "children's palace" (C: *tzu-kung*), "cinnabar cave," "jewel enclosure," or "red chamber" (C: *chu-shih*).

19 FALLOPIAN TUBES

Named after the Italian anatomist Gabriel Fallopio (1523–62), these two ovum-transporting tubes connect the ovaries (20) to the right and left upper ends of the uterus (18). The tubes guide the eggs from the ovaries toward the uterus. The meeting between ovum and sperm happens most often in the lower end of the fallopian tubes.

20 OVARIES

Part of the endocrine system, the two ovaries produce not only the eggs but also the hormones inhibin and relaxin, as well as sex hormones, such as estrogen, estradiol, and progesterone. The ovaries thus contribute to female embryonic development in general and to genital and sexual features in particular.

Ovary activity is controlled in a complex and synergetic fashion by the pituitary hormones FSH (follicle-stimulating hormone), LH (luteinizing hormone), and PRL(prolactin). Once a month during a woman's fertile years, a randomly selected ovum will float out of the ovaries and into one of the fallopian tubes (19), resulting either in fertilization (with appropriately timed intercourse) or in the monthly discharge of menstrual fluid. In China, the ovaries are considered to contain the female yin energy.

Beautiful color photographs of ovaries can be found in Lennart Nilsson's book *Behold Man*.

21 PERINEAL SPONGE

An area of sensitive tissue beneath the perineum (22) that fills with blood during sexual excitation.

22 PERINEUM

The female perineum, the flesh and skin in the area between the yoni and the anus, is not usually regarded as part of the genital system. However, for its exquisite receptivity to touch and for any sexual technique involving the muscles of the pelvic floor, its importance should not be overlooked.

According to the Chinese, the perineum and the ovaries (20) are together considered the seat of yin energy. The Sanskrit *yonisthana* (S: "yoni place") is seen as a center of subtle energy where the union of Shakti (goddess) and Shiva (god) takes place; the yonisthana is not far from where the kundalini is said to reside. In the sacred texts of India, the term *yonisthana* appears often, underlining the importance of this location and the attention paid to it.

In Western birthing practices the perineum is all too often unnecessarily cut in a procedure known as an episiotomy, in order to enlarge the vaginal/perineal opening to make room for the infant's head.

PELVIC-FLOOR MUSCLES

These muscles of the woman's genital area are sometimes referred to as love muscles. The pelvic floor consists of two groups of muscles, each of which can be activated and controlled independently. One group consists of the ischiocavernosus and bulbocavernosus muscles, and the musculus sphincter urethra, responsible for control of the urethra (13). The other group consists of the pubococcygeus or PC-muscle, the pubovaginalis, and the puborectalis.[▼] Besides the aforementioned muscles, the constrictor cunnis plays an important role in movements of the vagina.

I hope this brief description gives the reader a sense of the beauty and complexity of the female genital system. The perennial question regarding whether orgasms are vaginal, clitoral, or G-spot in nature becomes superfluous when we recognize the yoni as a completely interconnected and integrated whole.

[▼] The use and training of these muscles is discussed in various books on Taoist and Tantric sexual techniques, and under such varying names as *imsak, kabbazah,* pelvic-floor potential, or *pompoir.* See the author's *Encyclopedia of Erotic Wisdom* for more detail.

▼

Yoni Language: An Alphabetical Listing

Ace: Nineteenth-century England

Alembic: L: alchemist's code for uterus

Alley: Slang for vagina

Alpha and omega: G: "from beginning to end," "most important"

Beaver: Early twentieth-century United States

Bell: Since the 1940s, African-American slang for clitoris

Bhaga: S: "womb" or "vulva"

Black hole: Twentieth century, based on the black holes in physics

Blackness: Shakespeare, *Othello*

Boat : Shakespeare, *King Lear*

Bottomless pit: England

Box: Early twentieth-century United States

Boy in the boat: Lesbian slang for clitoris

Bread: Chaucer, *Canterbury Tales*

Bun: Seventeenth-century England

Bunny: Eighteenth-century England

Cabbage: Nineteenth-century England

Cake: Early twentieth-century England

Carnal trap: Seventeenth-century England

Cat: United States; see chat, pussy

Cave: Ancient China, eighteenth-century England

Cellar: England

Center of attraction: Eighteenth-century England, used by John Cleland in Fanny Hill

Center of bliss: Eighteenth-century England, used by John Cleland in Fanny Hill

Center of desire: Eighteenth-century England, used by John Cleland in Fanny Hill

Chalice: Code in Western esoteric schools

Chat: "Cat" (French); slang, like pussy

Chink: Nineteenth-century England

Chu-bin: J: middle vulva

Cinnabar cleft: Chinese/Taoist

Cinnabar hole: Chinese

Civet: From A: *zabad* (civet perfume)

Cleft: Seventeenth-century England

Con: French

Concha: L: for conch

Conno: Italian

Coño: Spanish

Cony: Sixteenth-century England for rabbit

Cookie: Twentieth-century United States

Cookies: Eighteenth-century England, for both yoni and labia

Counte: Old Middle English

Coyote: Nineteenth-century England

Crack: Sixteenth-century England

Cranny: Nineteenth-century England

Crease: Nineteenth-century United States

Crevice: Nineteenth-century England

Crown and feathers: Nineteenth-century England, for yoni and pubis

Crumpet: Nineteenth-century England (soft bread)

Cucurbite: L: alchemist's code

Cunnicle, Cunnikin: Nineteenth-century England, for vagina

Cunnus: L, from G: konnos

Cunt: English (c. fourteenth century), from cunnus

Cunte: Old Middle English

Cupid's alley: Nineteenth-century England, for vagina

Cupid's cave: Nineteenth-century England

Cupid's cloister: Nineteenth-century England

Cushion: Nineteenth-century England

Cut: Eighteenth-century England

Cwithe: Old English for womb

Cylinder: Early twentieth-century Australia

Cynthus: Alternative spelling of kunthus

Daisy: Nineteenth-century England

Dark gate: Chinese

Dead-end street: Canada

Delphos: G: "fish," "womb"

Ditch: Nineteenth-century England, for vagina

Doorway of Life: Chinese

Downy bit: Nineteenth-century England, for yoni and pubis

Drain: Nineteenth-century England, for vagina

El aride—El zeunbour: There are more than thirty Arabian names for various types of yoni. See chapter 7.

Eye: Sixteenth-century England, for vulva and vagina

Fanny: Eighteenth-century England, for yoni

Fiddle: Nineteenth-century England

Fig: Greek

Fish: Nineteenth-century England

Fish pond: Twentieth-century United States

Flap: Nineteenth-century England

Fleece: Eighteenth-century England, for pubic hair

Fleshy idol: Nineteenth-century England

Flower: Sixteenth-century England, mainly for hymen but sometimes for yoni

Flower of chivalry: Nineteenth-century England

Fruitful vine: Nineteenth-century England

Fufu: Manchurian

Furrow: Nineteenth-century England

Futz: Twentieth-century United States, probably from the German *Fotze*

Garden: Sixteenth-century England

Garden gate: Nineteenth-century
England, for vagina
Gash: Eighteenth-century England
Gate: Nineteenth-century England
Gate of jewels: Japanese for vagina
Ge-bin: J: low (rear) vulva
Genitals: L: *genitalis,* "birth"
Ghanta: S: "bell"
Gig: Seventeenth-century England; also
"loose woman," "mistress" (fourteenth
century)
Golden gate: Chinese
Golden gully: Chinese
Green grove, meadow: Nineteenth-
century England, for yoni and pubis
Grotto: Nineteenth-century England
Guhe : Common Nepali term, like our
vulva
Gully: Nineteenth-century England
Gunaikeios kteis: G: vulva

Happy valley: Twentieth-century
England
Heaven: Nineteenth-century England
Heavenly gate: Chinese
Hell: Eighteenth-century England
Hidden place: Chinese
Hoju: Japanese for clitoris
Hole of holes: Nineteenth-century
England, pun on "Holy of Holies"
Home sweet home: Nineteenth-
century England
Honeypot: Eighteenth-century
England
Hot lips: Nineteenth-century England,
for yoni and labia

Inner heart: Chinese
Ivory gate: Nineteenth-century England

Jade door: Chinese

Jade gate: Chinese
Jagad yoni: Sanskrit
Jaldri: Common Nepali term, like our
vulva
Jam: Nineteenth-century England
Janey: Twentieth-century, lesbian slang
Jelly roll: Twentieth-century United
States
Jo-bin: J: high (forward) vulva

Ka-t: E: "mother" as well as "yoni"
(literally, "the body of her")
Koilia: G: cavity, womb, yoni
Konnos: G: vulva
Kteis: G: yoni, scallop shell
Kunti: S: name of a Goddess and a term
for the yoni
Kunthus: G: name of a Goddess and a
term for the yoni
Kut: Dutch (slang)
Kvithe: Teutonic

Lap: Sixteenth-century England
Living fountain: Seventeenth-century
England
Lock: Eighteenth-century England
Long eye: Nineteenth-century England
Lotus of her wisdom: S: Tantric expres-
sion
Ludibria: L: from *ludibrium,* meaning
"shame" and "toy"

Maha Yoni: Sanskrit (see glossary)
Main avenue: Nineteenth-century
England
Man trap: Eighteenth-century England
Marble arch: Nineteenth-century
England, after the London monument
Mortar: Nineteenth-century England
Moss-rose: Nineteenth-century
England, for yoni and pubis

Mount Pleasant: Nineteenth-century England, based on mound of Venus

Muff: Seventeenth-century England

Mysterious gate: Chinese

Mysterious valley: Chinese

Mystic rose: Code, Western esoteric schools

Navel: Code used in the biblical Song of Songs

Nether eye: Fourteenth-century England

Nether lips: Nineteenth-century England, for labia majora

Nether mouth: Eighteenth-century England

Nonok: Bahasa Indonesian, slang

Noose: Twentieth century

Nursery: Nineteenth-century England

O: Seventeenth-century England

Oracle: Nineteenth-century England, from L: *orare,* "request"

Orange: Eighteenth-century England

Orchard: Sixteenth-century England

Orifice: Sixteenth-century England

Oyster: Nineteenth-century England

Padma: S: lotus

Papaya: Twentieth century

Paradise: Seventeenth-century England

Phoenix: Chinese

Pillow of musk: Chinese

Pit of darkness: Seventeenth-century England, for vagina

Pleasure garden: Seventeenth-century England

Precious crucible: Chinese/Taoist

Promised land: Nineteenth-century England

Pudendum: From L: *pudere,* "to be ashamed"

Pure lily: Chinese

Purple mushroom peak: Chinese

Pussy, puss: Seventeenth-century England

Qitbus: Gothic

Quaint: Modern spelling of queynthe

Queynthe: Code for cwithe

Quiff: Eighteenth-century England, variation on quim

Quim: Sixteenth century, based on Celtic *cwn,* "cleft," "valley"

Red ball: Chinese

Retort: Latin, alchemist's code

Rose: Eighteenth-century England

Secret cavern: Chinese

Sensitive cave: Chinese

Sex: Nineteenth-century England

Shrine of love: Nineteenth-century England

Slit: Seventeenth-century England

Snatch: Nineteenth-century England

Split: Nineteenth-century England

Split apricot: Nineteenth-century England

Squirrel: Twentieth-century United States

Star: Eighteenth-century England

Sugar basin: Nineteenth-century England, for vagina

Sulcus: L: "furrow"

Tidbit: Seventeenth-century England

Treasury: Sixteenth-century England

Trinket: Eighteenth-century England

Tunnel: Twentieth century

Turtle: Nineteenth-century England

Twat: Seventeenth-century England, "passage"

Two-leafed book: Renaissance, for labia

Vagina: L: "sheath"

Vagina dentata: L: "vagina with teeth"

Velvet sheath: Seventeenth-century England

Vent: Twentieth century

Vesica: code, L: "bladder"

Vulva: from L: "matrix" and "uterus"

Wound: Sixteenth-century England

Glossary

▼

Note: In the definitions, those words that appear in **boldface italics**
are defined elsewhere in the Glossary.

ANANGA RANGA

Written or compiled by the Indian author Kalyanamalla (sixteenth century), this
manual of erotic arts was first translated into English in 1873. Similarly to the ***Kama
Sutra,*** the ***Koka Shastra,*** and the *Ars Amatoria,* the *Ananga Ranga* covers a great
variety of erotic, sexual, and moral issues, from hygiene to incantations, from aphrodisiac love philters to sexual positions and the "how to" of seducing members of the
opposite gender. Although the *Kama Sutra* is the most famous among its competitors,
the *Ananga Ranga* is probably the better and more complete guide to the erotic ideas
and concepts of India. While the translation by Richard Burton (see bibliography) has
often been criticized as being insufficiently scientific, his many annotations and his
general knowledge of Oriental customs make this a valuable work.

BHAGA

A Sanskrit term with meanings that range from "luck," "happiness," and "wealth" to
"womb"; also a term for the yoni. Bhaga shares the same root word as bhagat (S: "devotee")
and bhagwan (S: "Divine One"), and is most often used in connection with the Goddess
and her major symbol. It also signifies that aspect of the human being that could be called
the divine enjoyer of things both erotic and nonerotic.

CORPUS CAVERNOSUM   (L: "body of caves")

In the past (pre-1987), *corpus cavernosum* was the term mainly used to indicate the
erectile part of the lingam, when this was not yet recognized as a male clitoris. Today the
term rightfully indicates nothing less than the erectile tissue that constitutes the shaft
and the two crura of the clitoris in both its female and its male forms. The corpus
cavernosum consists of involuntary muscles and a great number of cavities that become
filled with blood during arousal. This tissue can become nearly bone hard during sexual
excitement.

CORPUS SPONGIOSUM   (L: "spongy body")

Erectile tissue that makes up the clitoral crown (or glans), the bulbs below the labia
majora, and the urethral sponge. Different from the ***corpus cavernosum,*** this tissue
remains soft and elastic even when excited and erect.

CUPID

The Roman god of love, based on the Greek god Eros. Cupid is often depicted as a beautiful young man or boy with a bow and arrow.

G-SPOT

The popular term for a particularly sensitive area in the vagina, about halfway between the pubic bone and the cervix at the rear of the urethra. The G-spot is named after gynecologist Ernst Gräfenberg (1881–1957), who first put forth a theory concerning this area.

When authors Ladas, Whipple, and Perry first published their book *The G Spot* (1982), their findings on the existence of the "new" erogenous zone, and especially on its alleged ability to ejaculate an orgasmic fluid, were not officially recognized by most doctors and medical scientists. Leading scientific papers still do not publish the results of related research, thereby implicitly declaring the G-spot nonexistent (and themselves to be practically ignorant). Yet, a growing number of women and men know of the G-spot through experience and therefore do not need to be further convinced by medical data.

When the available evidence is reviewed, the conclusion must be drawn that there exists no actual G-spot in the sense in which it has been promoted, though its "discovery" certainly has led to a better understanding of what actually goes on in vaginal stimulation. The G-spot is a simple label for a rather complicated and sophisticated aspect of the yoni that is erotically sensitive and is also responsible for female ejaculation. For simplicity's sake the term G-spot can of course be used; however, disregarding the biological facts will only lead to new misconceptions. There can be no question that every woman possesses a G-spot. Whether or not she *feels* it depends on a wide variety of physical and psychological factors. Just as there are worlds of differences in the sensitivity of nipples and other standard erogenous zones, it is conceivable that not every woman is particularly sensitive in this area.

The area of the G-spot is actually the urethral sponge, an area of spongy tissue **(corpus spongiosum)** that also contains clusters of nerve endings, blood vessels, and paraurethral glands and ducts. The urethral sponge covers the female urethra (urinary tube) on all sides. During sexual stimulation provided by finger pressure or certain positions and movements of the lingam, the sponge can become engorged with blood, whereby it swells and becomes distinguishable to touch. A number of researchers in Israel and the United States have established that tissues of the G-spot area contain an enzyme also found in the male prostate glands, suggesting that the urethral sponge may be the female version of these glands, which are also rather sensitive to touch and pressure in men. The existence of these glands in this place may also explain the fluid secretions many women experience during or after G-spot stimulation.

For those not yet practically acquainted with this area, the G-spot presents an interesting paradox and invites adventurous exploration: in order to find it one has to stimulate it, and in order to stimulate it one has to find it! *Palace of yin* may have been an early Chinese term for the G-spot. Though the term is often used to simply mean "womb," it specifically refers to the location in the body where the orgasmic secretion called moon flower medicine lies waiting to be released. Given this, the Chinese may well have been the earliest discoverers of the G-spot, representing to us the ancients' insights into female ejaculation and the female prostate glands.

GUNAS

Indian philosophy holds that there are three basic ingredients or fundamental qualities of cosmos and being. All objects of the manifested world are thought to be composed of a particular mixture of the three gunas, which thus influence the unfoldment of all.

Tamas: The generalized principle of inertia and related phenomena, such as density, stability, and matter.

Rajas: The generalized principle of motion, activity, creativity, daring, and striving.

Sattva: The generalized principle of order, including time and structure.

HAJJ

The Koran states: "And proclaim unto mankind the Pilgrimage, they will come to thee on foot and on every lean camel."[1] To take part in the hajj at least once in his or her life is the wish and duty of every Muslim. Arriving at the Kaaba, Muslims pray, weep, surrender, and pray again. They perform the **tawaf** and drink of the holy water of the *zamzam* (sacred well). The lucky ones carry home a costly shred of the beautiful black *kiswa*, the cloth that covers the shrine. Though not all in the huge crowd succeed, everyone will try to kiss or at least touch the sacred meteorite in order to partake of its divine energy. When John Ferguson writes "to kiss the Black Stone is to kiss God's right hand"[2] he certainly captures the spirit of the occasion (except for the fact that the stone does not seem to be a hand). That such a ritual both imparts life energy to the faithful worshipers and serves to empower the sacred object even more is aptly expressed in these lines of the famous mystical poet Ibn 'Arabi (1165–1240): "Behold the secret building before it is too late, and you will see it take on life through those who circle round it and walk round its stone."

Today, with millions of pilgrims visiting the Kaaba annually, the hajj has become a major exercise in logistics and features prominently in the budget of Saudi Arabia. Airport extensions cost $200 million, the Great Mosque was enlarged for another $155 million, and an annual sum of about $45 million is spent for the event itself.[3] The affluent guardians of the shrine dig deep into their pockets so that every one of the faithful can see, feel, touch, or kiss the hand of Allah.

JAGAD YONI

A **Sanskrit** term meaning "universal Yoni" or "the great cosmic Vulva of space/time." The term is used as a title of honor for the goddess Shakti as Mother of All. It is based on the word *jagad*, sanskrit for "universe," or "world."

KAMA SUTRA (S: "Aphorisms of Love")

A work on Indian sexual morals and techniques that can be likened to contemporary sex manuals. Compiled by Vatsyayana (third/fourth century C.E.) "in modesty and supreme reverence," the *Kama Sutra* combines concepts, knowledge, and wisdom of the Indian erotic arts from the time between 1000 B.C.E. and 400 C.E. First translated into English in 1883, ten years after the **Ananga Ranga,** the *Kama Sutra* has become the most famous of all Indian erotic works.

KOKA SHASTRA

This is the popular name for an early medieval erotic textbook written by the Indian author Kokkoka (twelfth century), thus its title, translating as "the scripture (shastra) of Koka." The text's true and original title is *Ratirahasya,* a Sanskrit word translating as "the secrets of Rati," Rati being an Indian goddess of love. The *Koka Shastra* is the medieval equivalent of the **Kama Sutra,** and the author looks back with nostalgic reverence to those times. A comparison of these texts yields much information about the changes that have taken place in Indian society during the intervening nine centuries.

MAHA YONI (S: "great Yoni")

A term used for the Yoni of the Goddess and for that moment during a secret Yoni Puja (see chapter 4) when the living woman's yoni, charged and ready to receive the lingam, is truly energized and thus transformed into a manifestation of the Goddess and her Yoni.

PERFUMED GARDEN

An Arabic erotic manual, comparable to the Indian **Kama Sutra,** written by the Tunisian Sheikh al-Nefzaoui (sixteenth century) and translated into English by Sir Richard Burton in 1866.

The text begins by praising God as well as the human genitals: "Praise be given to Allah who has placed man's greatest pleasure in the natural parts of woman and has destined the natural parts of man to afford the greatest enjoyment to woman." Apart from telling a number of erotic fairy tales, the book goes on to name, explain, and describe twenty-five coital positions and techniques. At the end of this section the author adds, "If there be anybody who thinks that those which I have described are not exhaustive, he has only to look for new ones."

The Perfumed Garden also contains a large collection of yoni and lingam terminology. Besides the Arabic names and their translations, it describes thirty-five types of lingams and thirty-eight types of yonis in terms that often afford insights into the psyches and behavior of males and females of that culture and era. Though the work is clearly written by a man and mainly for men, its author realizes that women have differing sexual tastes and preferences. He often admonishes his readers to find out which kind of union the woman prefers most and to help her reach satisfaction and fulfillment.

SANSKRIT

The sacred language of Hinduism, and the language in which most Hindu religious texts are written. The term itself (S: *samskrta*) means "perfect and complete," an appropriate description for what is also known as a "language of the gods" or devanagari. As Sanskrit developed alongside the philosophical, scientific, and religious thought of India, it features highly differentiated and sophisticated terminology for subtle physiology, mental/spiritual processes, and extraordinary states of consciousness for which no immediate equivalents are known in Western languages. This not only makes for a challenge in translation but also presents possibilities for learning from a very sophisticated language and culture.

The written language consists of approximately fifty glyphs or letters that are often difficult to transliterate into Latin-based Western languages. Several transliteration systems are in use.

SHAKTA

One of the five major religious systems of Hinduism, Shakta (also called Shaktism in Western literature) designates the worship of the goddess Shakti as the principal deity and energy of the universe and creation. The creative force, recognized as being sexual in nature, is therefore—similar to Tantric practice—often represented in images of sexual union. Different subschools may employ teachings that mirror this on the physical plane by using sexuality in their rituals; others see it as mere symbology and reject all actual union. One feature that clearly delineates the difference between **Tantra** and Shakta is the fact that Shakta teachings always regard the feminine principle as supreme, whereas in Tantra devotees are free to choose whether to direct themselves to a male or a female deity.

SHINGON

An esoteric school of Japanese Buddhism. Its name, which translates as "the True Word," is a Japanese translation of the **Sanskrit** *mantrayana*. The school was founded in 808 by Kobo Daishi (774–835), also known by his earlier name of Kukai. Kukai spent two and one-half years in China studying the Chinese translations of the newly arrived esoteric teachings of Indian Buddhism and **Tantra.** He studied and practiced with masters of the Mi-tsung (C: "School of Secrets"), a school that was never to gain a strong foothold in China. Through Kukai those teachings reached Japan, where today Shingon is one of the largest Buddhist schools.

Although Shingon teachings are divided into *ken-kyo* (exoteric teachings) and *mitsou-kyo* (esoteric teachings), it was mainly the latter that interested Kukai. Esoteric rituals, practices, and teachings are predominant is Shingon. Similar to Tibetan Tantra, Shingon makes use of mandalas (paintings) and mudras (gestures), and holds the *vajra* (scepter) as a sacred object. More than three centuries after Kobo Daishi's death, the specifically sexual teachings were slowly meted out by the school's leadership. Those who disagreed with this development branched off and founded the **Tachikawa Ryu,** a school in which they continued the sexual teachings and practices.

SHINTO

A Chinese term for the indigenous, nature-oriented Japanese religion Kami-no-Michi, which translates as "the Way of the Divine." Its main *kami* (J: "deity," "spirit") is the goddess Amaterasu, representing the sun; its major shrine is at Ise, near Kyoto. Though there are at least 130 different sects, Japan also knew a so-called state Shinto, which was suppressed by the post-war American administration.

Other important Shinto deities are the goddess Ama-no-Uzume and the creation deities Izanami and Izanagi.

TACHIKAWA RYU

A Japanese Tantric sect, corresponding to the Indian left-handed Tantra, founded in 1114 by Nin-kan (1057—1123) as a branch of **Shingon.** Nin-kan taught that sexual union and one's living body were a means for directly obtaining Buddhahood; the Tachikawa held mass meetings where Tantric rites were practiced. Although the Tachikawa Ryu was soon outlawed by the authorities, it continued covertly until at least 1689; according to John Stevens, it is still active today.[4]

Because of the involvement of sexuality in their rituals, the sect still has a rather bad name in Japan, and most of their texts are hidden away in one or more monasteries, "securely sealed and marked with the century-old notice *ake-bekarazu*" (in English, "Do Not Open!").[5]

One of the few known Tachikawa texts is *The Sutra Proclaiming the Secret Method Enabling a Man and a Woman to Experience the Bliss of Buddhahood in This Very Body.* The text is excerpted in John Stevens's book *Lust for Enlightenment,* and lists, among other things, a classification of different kinds of human genitals.

TANTRA

The meaning of this Sanskrit term can best be approximated by such concepts as "continuum," "web," and "context"; such ambiguity has led to many different translations and definitions of Tantra. The term itself refers to a particular religious tradition with its roots in India, as well as to a sacred text within that school of thought.

Historically, Tantra originated in approximately the fifth century and reached its peak of social diffusion by about 1200. Tantra seems to have originally been a kind of religious and social revolt against foreign invaders—the Aryan peoples with their patriarchal priests and male deities. With its roots in pre-Aryan, Indian spirituality, Tantra reestablished the tradition of the Great Goddess (Shakti, Kali) and infused what is generally called Hinduism with ancient aboriginal, tribal practices and beliefs. Certain provinces of India, the mother country of Tantra, have made outstanding contributions to the development of Tantra. Among these Bengal and Assam are most noteworthy; however, Kerala and Kashmir can also be considered as historically Tantric regions. Tantra continues to influence Indian life and ritual today.

As a religious tradition, Tantra is a mystical/spiritual and nondualist system of psychology, philosophy, and cosmology that assumes the union of opposites on all levels of being and becoming—from cosmic to quantum levels and on astral, mental, and physical planes. This central theme is expressed in most of its sacred texts, as well as in its practices of alchemy and science and its works of art. The same applies to the ritual observances practiced by Tantrics of both genders. Women and men are seen as microcosmic expressions of the goddess Shakti and the god Shiva. The aim in actual practice is therefore to go beyond any duality and once more achieve original union.

Tantra has penetrated and thus influenced many other religious schools, and therefore comes in several varieties. Apart from the original Indian (Hindu) Tantra, and the Tibetan (Buddhist) form it brought forth, there are also Chinese, Japanese, and even Western schools of Tantra (for example, the sexual magick of Aleister Crowley and the intimacy training of Bhagwan and Osho).

The various schools of Tantric thought are classified as either left-handed (S: *vamacara*) or right-handed (S: *daksinacara*). Explaining the precise differences between these schools is beyond the scope of this book. In general it can be said that vamacara is the old school in which the sexual current is employed on a physical level, while daksinacara is the tempered school in which sexual energy is employed on a level of symbolism and visualization only.

The term Tantra can also be used to designate a sacred treatise containing spiritual and psychophysical teachings concerned with the transmutation of energy, liberation of the mind, attainment of one's full potential, and other practices that belong to the school of thought known as Tantra. The balanced union of opposites is considered by Tantrics to be a sure way of achieving liberation of mind and body, a liberation from the supposedly endless cycle of unconscious rebirth. In order to facilitate such union on all levels of being, Tantra makes use of a variety of physiological, psychological, and devotional/spiritual techniques, many of which have been described in my books[6] and in other specialized works.[7]

TAWAF AL-QUDUM

Every pilgrim, male and female, who comes to visit the Great Mosque at Mecca is required to take part in the ritual tawaf. This involves seven circumambulations of the Kaaba, starting at the corner where the meteorite is situated and moving counterclockwise. Barefoot on the hot, sunsoaked marble, the pilgrim has to do the first three rounds at a slow run and the last four rounds in a measured walk. Unknowingly, these pilgrims follow the ancient ritual of the seven priestesses of Al'Uzza.

Gerald Hawkins points out that this may mean "three circuits for the fast moving Moon, Mercury and Venus, and four for the sun and the planets Mars, Jupiter and Saturn."[8] Each round ends with a prayer to Allah, which is said at the black stone.

VULVA

Properly used, the term *vulva* refers to the more or less visible, outer parts of the yoni that surround the opening of the vagina. However, the term is also erroneously used for either the uterus (womb) or the vagina (the tube between the vulva and the uterus).

YANG

One aspect of the Chinese concept of yin/yang, an expression of the omnipresent dual forces at work in the universe and all of creation. Among numerous other associations, yang represents the energy that manifests as male, light, heaven, and positive (in the sense of magnetic polarity or electrical charge).

YIN

The other aspect of the Chinese concept of yin/yang, an expression of the omnipresent dual forces at work in the universe and in all of creation. Among numerous other associations, yin represents the energy that manifests as female, dark, earth, and negative (in the sense of magnetic polarity or electrical charge).

YONI TANTRA

The Yoni Tantra is a religious text from Bengal mainly concerned with describing the Yoni Puja, or "Mass of the Vulva," one of the more secret and esoteric Tantric rituals dedicated to creating and consuming the sacred fluid yonitattva.

According to this text, sexual union is an indispensable part of Tantric ritual and may be performed by and with all women between the ages of twelve and sixty years, married or not, except for a virgin. The text explicitly forbids the incestuous mother/son constellation.

In general, however, this Tantra does not impose many restrictions on the practitioner (S: *sadhaka*) who is dedicated to the Yoni Puja. It advocates the use of wine and physical union, and leaves the choice of partner, place, and time much up to the practitioner. Nevertheless, the male sadhaka is explicitly admonished "never to ridicule a Yoni" and to treat all women well and never be offensive toward them.

ZAP-LAM   (T: "profound path")

A fulfillment-process yoga practiced by Yeshe Tsogyal in Bhutan with her two yogin partners, as well as by many of the high initiates of Tibetan Tantra. It has been described as "the yoga of co-incident emptiness and pleasure on the profound path,"[9] in which sexual energy is used as motivation and desire as the object of meditation, both of which are then transformed into awareness (T: *ye-shes*) and pure pleasure (T: *bde-chen*).

The technique of zap-lam can be properly carried out only by adepts trained in the control of all levels of energy, and especially in the conscious retraction of the blended male and female seed essence (T: *thig-le*, S: *bodhicitta*). In order to practice zap-lam, the practitioner is expected to have received the Wisdom Initiation (S: *prajnajnana-abhiseka*) and all those initiations preceding it.

NOTES

▼

INTRODUCTION

1. Achad, *Hymns to the Star Goddess.*
2. Daniélou, *The Phallus.*
3. Bolen, *Goddesses in Everywoman.*
4. Stone, *Ancient Mirrors of Woman-hood.*

CHAPTER 1

1. Neumann, *The Great Mother,* 85.
2. Tannahill, *Sex in History,* 42.
3. Ibid.
4. Leroi-Gourhan, *Préhistoire de l'art occidental,* 461.
5. Ibid., 340.

CHAPTER 2

1. Hall, *Moon and the Virgin,* 44.

CHAPTER 3

1. King, *Tantra for Westerners.*

CHAPTER 4

1. Schoterman, *Yoni Tantra,* 11.
2. Banerjee, *A Brief History of Tantra Literature,* 339.
3. Majupuria, *Nepalese Women,* 25.
4. Mullin, *Selected Works of the Dalai Lama II,* 107.
5. Ibid., 107f.
6. Ibid., 137.
7. Douglas and Slinger, *Sexual Secrets,* 126.

8. Mullin, 146.
9. Payne, *The Tantric Ritual of Japan,* 36.
10. Brhad Aranyika Upanishad, VI (4.3) as quoted in Payne, 47.
11. Payne, 36.
12. Ibid.
13. Allegro, *Sacred Mushroom and the Cross,* 221.

CHAPTER 5

1. Waley, *Lao-Tzu,* 159.
2. Briffault, *The Mothers.*
3. Tsogyal, *The Life and Liberation of Padmasambhava* and *The Lotus-Born.*
4. Ibid.
5. Ibid.
6. Artist and researcher Winifred M. Lubell, *The Metamorphosis of Baubo,* and psychologist Georges Devereux, *Baubo.*
7. Andersen, *The Witch on the Wall.*
8. Weir and Jerman, *Images of Lust.*

CHAPTER 6

1. Mookerjee, *Kali,* 32.
2. Ibid.
3. Ibid, 31.
4. Bhattacharyya, Douglas, and Slinger, *The Path of the Mystic Lover.*

5. Bhattacharyya, 170.

6. Dowman, *Sky Dancer,* 71.

7. Marglin, *Types of Sexual Union,* 310.

8. Snellgrove in Shaw, *Women in Tantric Buddhism,* 250.

9. Ibid.

10. Henricks, *La-Tzu.*

11. Radhakrishnan, *The Principal Upanishads,* 321f.

CHAPTER 7

1. George, *The Candamaharosana Tantra,* 54.

2. Mookerjee and Khanna, 200.

3. Burton, *Kama Sutra and Perfumed Garden.*

4. Stevens, *Lust for Enlightenment.*

5. van Gulik, Sexual Life in Ancient China, 273.

6. Burton, *Kama Sutra and Perfumed Garden*

CHAPTER 8

1. Schneeman, in Gadon, *Once and Future Goddess,* 295.

2. Text from the musical meditation *Blues for Memphis Slim,* published (1970) on *Eric Burdon declares "War,"* Avenue Records/Far Out Productions.

3. Nin, *Delta of Venus,* 170.

4. *Marie Claire* (Dutch edition), July 1995, 48.

5. See Chicago, *The Dinner Party,* for a detailed visual and textual report on this work.

6. Denish, *Fiery Drippings,* 28.

7. See for example the personal accounts in *Modern Primitives* edited by Vale and Juno or the more scientific publication *Marks of Civilization* by Arnold Rubin. Other relevant information is available on the Internet and through specialized videos.

APPENDIX I: YONI TOPOGRAPHY

1. For an example, see Hafez and Evans, *The Human Vagina* (2 vols.); and W. C. Younge, *Sex and Internal Secretions* (2 vols).

2. Lowndes-Sevely, *Eve's Secrets,* 15.

3. Ibid, 25.

4. Richter, *Sexual Slang.*

5. El Saadawi, *Vrouwen in de Arabische wereld,* 26.

6. Lowndes-Sevely.

GLOSSARY

1. The Koran, 22:27.

2. Ferguson, *An Illustrated Encyclopaedia of Mysticism,* 83.

3. Guellouz, *Pilgrimage to Mecca.*

4. Stevens, *Lust for Enlightenment.*

5. van Gulik, 359.

6. Camphausen, *The Divine Library* and *The Encyclopedia of Erotic Wisdom.*

7. See Banerjee, Chia, Comfort, Douglas and Slinger, George, Ramsdale, and Rawson in bibliography.

8. Hawkins, *Mindsteps to the Cosmos,* 167.

9. Dowman, 249.

BIBLIOGRAPHY

NONFICTION

Achad, Frater. *Hymns to the Star Goddess*. Chicago: Will Ransom, 1923.

Adler, Margot. *Drawing Down the Moon*. Boston: Beacon, 1981.

Allegro, John M. *The Sacred Mushroom and the Cross*. London: Sphere, 1973.

Andersen, Jørgen. *The Witch on the Wall: Medieval Erotic Sculpture in the British Isles*. Copenhagen: Rosenkilde & Bagger, 1977.

Banerjee, S. C. *A Brief History of Tantra Literature*. Calcutta: Naya Prokash, 1988.

Bhattacharyya, Bhaskar, Nik Douglas, and Penny Slinger. *The Path of the Mystic Lover: Baul Songs of Passion and Ecstasy*. Rochester, Vt.: Inner Traditions, 1993.

Blank, Joani, ed. *Femalia*. San Francisco: Down There Press, 1993.

Bolen, Jean Shinoda. *Goddesses in Everywoman*. San Francisco: Harper & Row, 1984.

Branston, Brian. *Gods of the North*. London: Thames & Hudson, 1980.

———. *Lost Gods of England*. London: Thames & Hudson, 1974.

Briffault, Robert. *The Mothers: A Study of the Origins of Sentiments and Institutions*. 3 vols. London: Allen & Unwin, 1927.

Bunch, Bryan, and Alexander Hellemans. *The Timetables of Technology*. New York: Simon & Schuster, 1994.

Burton, Sir Richard. *The Illustrated Kama Sutra, Ananga Ranga, Perfumed Garden*. Rochester, Vt.: Park Street Press, 1991.

———. *Kama Sutra and Perfumed Garden*. Hertfordshire, England: Omega (n.d.).

———. *A Personal Narrative of a Pilgrimage to Al-Medinah and Mecca*. London: 1856.

Buruma, Ian. *Behind the Mask*. New York: New American Library, 1985.

Camphausen, Rufus C. *De heilige steen van Mekka*. Amsterdam: Bres #139, 1989.

———. *The Encyclopedia of Erotic Wisdom*. Rochester, Vt.: Inner Traditions, 1991.

———. *The Divine Library*. Rochester, Vt.: Inner Traditions, 1992.

Charles-Picard, G. *The Larousse Encyclopedia of Archaeology*. London: Hamlin, 1983.

Chia, Mantak, and Maneewan Chia. *Healing Love Through the Tao: Cultivating Female Sexual Energy*. Huntington N.Y.: Healing Tao Books, 1986.

Chicago, Judy. *The Dinner Party: A Symbol of Our Heritage*. Garden City, N.Y.: Anchor Books, 1979.

Chou Tz'u-Chi. *Lao Tzu Ka'o-Shu*. Taipei: Fu-Ven T'u-Shu, 1984.

Comfort, Alex. *Koka Shastra*. London: Allen & Unwin, 1984.

Daniélou, Alain. *The Phallus: Sacred Symbol of Male Creative Power*. Rochester, Vt.: Inner Traditions, 1995.

———, trans. *The Complete Kama Sutra*. Rochester, Vt.: Inner Traditions, 1994.

Dawood, N. J. *The Koran*. Harmondsworth, England: Penguin, 1974.

Delaney, Janice, M. J. Lupton, and E. Toth. *The Curse: A Cultural History of Menstruation*. Urbana, Ill.: University of Illinois, 1988.

Denish. *Fiery Drippings from Her Sacrificial Vessel*. India: Private publication, 1984.

———. *Mahasangama Tantra, Sri Cinnamasta*. Amsterdam: Private publication, 1990.

Devereux, Georges. *Baubo: Die Mythische Vulva*. Frankfurt am Main: Syndikat, 1981.

Douglas, Nik, and Penny Slinger. *Sexual Secrets: Alchemy of Ecstasy*. Rochester, Vt.: Inner Traditions, 1979.

Dowman, Keith. *Sky Dancer: The Secret Life and Songs of Lady Yeshe Tsogyal*. London: Routledge & Kegan Paul, 1984.

Duca, Lo. *Erotik im Fernen Osten*. Wiesbaden: Verlag Modernes Antiquariat, 1967.

Eisler, Riane. *The Chalice and the Blade: Our History, Our Future*. New York: HarperCollins, 1988.

Eros in Antiquity. New York: Erotic Art Book Society, 1978.

Fabricius, Johannes. *Alchemy: Medieval Alchemists and their Royal Art*. Wellingborough: Aquarian Press, 1989.

Ferguson, John. *An Illustrated Encyclopaedia of Mysticism*. London: Thames & Hudson, 1976.

Fester, Richard, et al. *Vrouw en macht: Vijf miljoen jaren oergeschiedenis van de vrouw*. Helmond, the Netherlands: Uitgeverij Helmond, 1980.

Frazier, Nancy. *Georgia O'Keeffe*. New York: Crescent, 1990.

Frymer-Kensky, Tikva. *In the Wake of the Goddess: Women, Culture and the Biblical Transformation of Pagan Myth*. New York: Ballantine, 1993.

Gadon, Elinor W. *The Once and Future Goddess: A Symbol for Our Time*. Wellingborough: Aquarian, 1990.

George, Christopher S., trans. *The Candamaharosana Tantra*. American Oriental Series, no. 56. New Haven: American Oriental Society, 1974.

Getty, Adele. *The Goddess: Mother of Living Nature*. London: Thames & Hudson, 1990.

Gimbutas, Marija. *Goddesses and Gods of Old Europe*. London: Thames & Hudson, 1984.

————. *The Language of the Goddess.* San Francisco: Harper & Row, 1989.

Guellouz, Ezzedine, and Frikha. *Pilgrimage to Mecca.* The Hague: East/West Publications, 1980.

Haeckel, Ernst. *Art Forms in Nature.* New York: Dover, 1974.

Hafez, E. S. E., and T. N. Evans, eds. *The Human Vagina*, 2 vols. Amsterdam and New York: North Holland Publishing Company, 1978.

Hall, Nor. *The Moon and the Virgin.* New York: Harper & Row, 1984.

Hawkins, Gerald S. *Mindsteps to the Cosmos.* San Francisco: Harper & Row, 1983.

Hawley, J. Stratton, and Donna M. Wulff. *Divine Consort: Radha and the Goddesses of India.* Delhi: Motilal, 1982.

Henricks, Robert G. *La-Tzu: Te-Tao King: A New Translation Based on the Recently Discovered Ma-wang Tui Texts.* New York: Ballantine, 1989.

Iglehart-Austen, Hallie. *The Heart of the Goddess: Art, Myth, and Meditations of the World's Sacred Feminine.* Berkeley: Wingbow Press, 1990.

Jackson, D., and J. Jackson. *Tibetan Thangka Paintings.* London: Serindia Publications, 1994.

King, Francis. *Tantra for Westerners.* Wellingborough: Aquarian Press, 1986.

Knight, Chris. *Blood Relations: Menstruation and the Origins of Culture.* New Haven: Yale University Press, 1991.

Knight, R. P., & T. Wright. *Sexual Symbolism: A History of Phallic Worship.* New York: Julian Press 1962.

Ladas, Alice Khan, Beverly Whipple, and John D. Perry. *The G-Spot and Other Recent Discoveries about Human Sexuality.* New York: Holt, Rinehart, & Winston, 1982.

Lander, Louise. *Images of Bleeding: Menstruation as Ideology.* New York: Orlando, 1988.

Leroi-Gourhan, André. *Préhistoire de l'art occidental.* Paris: Editions d'art Lucien Mazenod, 1971.

Lowndes-Sevely, Josephine. *Eve's Secrets: A Revolutionary Perspective on Human Sexuality.* London: Collins, 1987.

Lubell, Winifred Milius. *The Metamorphosis of Baubo: Myths of Woman's Sexual Energy.* Nashville: Vanderbilt University Press, 1994.

Mackey, Mary. *The Year the Horses Came.* New York: Onyx/Dutton, 1995.

Majupuria, Indra. *Nepalese Women.* Kathmandu: M. Devi, 1982.

Mani, Vettam. *Puranic Encyclopedia: A Comprehensive Dictionary with Special Reference to the Epic and Puranic Literature.* Delhi: Motilal Banarsidass, 1975.

Marglin, Frederique Apffel. "Types of Sexual Union and Their Implicit Meanings." In

Divine Consort: Radha and the Goddesses of India. Delhi: Motilal, 1982.

Mookerjee, Ajit. *Kali: The Feminine Force.* Rochester, Vt.: Destiny Books, 1988.

———. *Tantra Asana: A Way to Self-Realization.* Basel: Ravi Kumar, 1971.

Mookerjee, Ajit, and Madhu Khanna. *Tantric Way: Art, Science, Ritual.* London: Thames & Hudson, 1977.

Mullin, Glenn. *Selected Works of the Dalai Lama II: Tantric Yogas of Sister Niguma.* Ithaca, N.Y.: Snow Lion, 1985.

Muthesius, Angelika, and Gilles Neret. *Erotiek in de kunst.* Cologne: Taschen/Librero, 1993.

Neumann, Erich. *The Great Mother: An Analysis of the Archetype.* London: Routledge & Kegan Paul, 1963.

Nilsson, Lennart. *Behold Man: A Photographic Journey Inside the Body.* Boston: Little Brown, 1974.

Osman, Sarah Ann. *Heilige Plaatsen.* Rijswijk, the Netherlands: Elmar, 1990.

Owen, Lara. *Her Blood Is Gold: Celebrating the Power of Menstruation.* San Francisco: Harper-Collins, 1993.

Payne, Richard Karl. *The Tantric Ritual of Japan: Feeding the Gods—the Shingon Fire Ritual.* Delhi: Aditya, 1991.

Radhakrishnan, S. *The Principal Upanishads.* New York: Harper and Brothers, 1953.

Ramsdale, David and Ellen. *Sexual Energy Ecstasy,* rev. ed. Playa del Ray, Calif.: Peak Skill, 1991.

Rawson, Philip. *Art of Tantra.* London: Thames and Hudson, 1973.

Rice, Edward. *Eastern Definitions.* Garden City, N.Y.: Doubleday, 1978.

Richter, Alan. *Sexual Slang.* New York: HarperCollins, 1995.

Rubin, Arnold. *Marks of Civilization.* Los Angeles: Museum of Cultural History, 1988.

Saadawi, Nawal El. *Gesluierde Eva. Vrouwen in de Arabische wereld.* Amsterdam, the Netherlands: Mutinga, 1989.

Schoterman, J. A. *Yoni Tantra.* New Delhi: Manohar, 1980.

Scott, George R. *Phallic Worship: A History of Sex and Sex Rites.* London: Luxor, 1966.

Shaw, Miranda. *Passionate Enlightenment: Women in Tantric Buddhism.* Princeton: Princeton University Press, 1994.

Shuttle, Penelope, and Peter Redgrove. *The Wise Wound: Menstruation and Everywoman.* London: Collins, 1986.

Sjöö, Monica, and Barbara Mor. *The Great Cosmic Mother.* San Francisco: Harper & Row, 1987.

Stevens, John. *Lust for Enlightenment: Buddhism and Sex*. Boston: Shambhala, 1990.

Stone, Merlin. *Ancient Mirrors of Womanhood: A Treasury of Goddess and Heroine Lore from Around the World*. Boston: Beacon Press, 1979.

———. *The Paradise Papers*. London: Virago, 1976.

Stubbs, Kenneth Ray, and C. D. Chasen. *Clitoral Kiss: A Fun Guide to Oral Sex for Men and Women*. Larkspur, Calif.: Secret Garden, 1993.

Talalaj, J., and S. Talaj. *Human Sex, Ceremonies and Customs*. Melbourne: Hill of Content Publishing, 1994.

Tannahill, Reay. *Sex in History*. London: Hamish Hamilton, 1980.

Taylor, Dena. *Red Flower: Rethinking Menstruation*. Freedom, Calif.: Crossing Press, 1988.

Taylor, G. Rattrey. *Sex in History—de zeden in het verleden*. Amsterdam: Allert de Lange, 1965.

Tiwari, Jagdish Narain. *Goddess Cults in Ancient India (0-700 a.d.)*. Delhi: Sundeep Prakashan, 1985.

Tsogyal, Yeshe. *The Life and Liberation of Padmasambhava*. 2 vols. Translated by Kenneth Douglas and Gwendoyn Bays. Berkeley: Dharma, 1978.

———. *The Lotus-Born: The Life Story of Padmasambhava*. Translated by Erik Pema Kunsang. Boston: Shambhala, 1993.

Vale, V., and Andrea Juno. *Modern Primitives: Tattoo—Piercing—Scarification*. San Francisco: Re/Search, 1989.

van Gulik, Robert H. *Sexual Life in Ancient China*. Leiden, the Netherlands: Brill, 1974.

Vermaseren, Marten J. *Cybele and Attis*. London: Thames and Hudson, 1977.

Vorberg, Gaston. *Ars Erotica Veterum*. Hanau, Germany: Müller & Kiepenheuer, 1968.

Waley, Arthur, trans. *Lao-Tzu: The Way and Its Power. A Study of the Tao Te Ching and Its Place in Chinese Thought*. London: Allen & Unwin, 1977.

Weir, Anthony, and James Jerman. *Images of Lust: Sexual Carvings on Medieval Churches*. London: Batsford, 1986.

Wile, Douglas. *The Art of the Bedchamber: Chinese Sexual Yoga Classics, Including Women's Solo Meditation Texts*. New York: SUNY, 1992.

Young, Serinity, ed. *An Anthology of Sacred Texts by and about Women*. London: Pandora, 1993.

Younge, W. C. ed. *Sex and Internal Secretions*. 2 vols. Baltimore: Williams & Wilkins, 1961.

FICTION

These books include descriptions of people and/or rituals connected to worship of the Yoni or veneration of the Goddess in general.

Auel, J. M. *The Clan of the Cave Bear.* London: Hodder & Stoughton, 1980.

——. The *Valley of Horses.* New York: Bantam, 1982.

——. *The Mammoth Hunters.* New York: Bantam, 1985.

——. *The Plains of Passage.* London: Hodder & Stoughton, 1990.

Bradley, Marion. *Firebrand.* New York: Pocket Books, 1988.

——. *The Mists of Avalon.* London: Sphere, 1984.

——. *The Ruins of Isis.* New York: Pocket Books, 1979.

Burgess, Anthony. *Kingdom of the Wicked.* New York: Pocket Books, 1985.

Farmer, Philip José. *Hadon of Ancient Opar.* New York: Daw Books, 1974.

——. *Flight to Opar.* New York: Daw Books, 1976.

——. *A Feast Unknown.* London: Quartet Books, 1975.

——. *Strange Relations.* London: Panther, 1966.

Fortune, Dion. *The Sea Priestess.* York Beach, Me.: Weiser, 1985.

Giroux, Leo. *Rishi.* London: Collins, 1985.

Grant, Joan. *Winged Pharao.* New York: Berkley, 1977.

Herley, Richard. *Pagans.* London: Grafton, 1986.

Llywelyn, Morgan. *The Horse Goddess.* New York: Pocket Books, 1983.

Mackey, Mary. *Last Warrior Queen.* London: Unwin, 1985.

Mailer, Norman. *Ancient Evenings.* London: Picador, 1984.

Merritt, Abraham. *Ship of Ishtar.* New York: Avon, 1973.

Renault, Mary. *The Bull from the Sea.* Harmondsworth, England: Penguin, 1983.

——. *The King Must Die.* New York: Bantam, 1981.

Rider Haggard, H. *She.* New York: Ball, 1978.

——. *Ayesha: Return of She.* New York: Ball, 1978.

——. *She and Allan.* New York: Ball, 1978.

——. *Wisdom's Daughter.* New York: Ball, 1978.

Silverberg, Robert. *Gilgamesh the King.* London: Pan, 1986.

Thomas, Elizabeth Marshall. *Reindeer Moon.* London: Collins, 1987.

——. *Animal Wife.* New York: Pocket Books, 1990.

Van Lustbader, Eric. *White Ninja.* New York: Fawcett Crest, 1990.

Watson, Ian. *The Book of the River.* New York: Daw, 1984.

——. *The Book of the Stars.* London: Panther, 1986.

——. *The Whores of Babylon.* London: Grafton, 1988

ILLUSTRATION CREDITS

▼

Page ii, Figure 1: *Wood Yoni*, carved from a single trunk of a sacred palm, from tribal Andhra Pradesh, India, c. 1900. Height 53.3 cm. Photograph courtesy of Nik Douglas, copyright 1971 and 1996.

Page iii, Figure 2: *Kali Yoni*. Painting by Denish, 1986. Gouache, 50 cm. x 50 cm.

Page v, Figure 3: *Sacred Triangle*. Drawing by Christina Camphausen, 1995. Color pencil on paper, 20 cm. x 20 cm.

Page vi. Figure 4: Crater in the Tongariro National Park, New Zealand. Photograph by Ton Kocken, 1988.

Page viii. Figure 5: *Yin Yin*. Drawing by Christina Camphausen, 1995. Pencil on paper, 10.5 cm. x 10.5 cm.

Figure 6: Twelfth-century stone carving from the Sixty-Four Yogini Temple. Archeological Survey of India

Figure 7: Rock painting at Nourlangie Rock, Alligator River, Arnhem Land, Northern Territory, Australia. Photograph by Robert Edwards, courtesy of the Aboriginal Arts Board, Australian Consulate General, New York.

Figure 8: Bas-relief from Nimes, France. Musée de l'Art Histoire, Nimes.

Figure 9: Stone carving from Moigny cave, Île-de-France (Fester, *Vrouw en macht*).

Figure 10: Emblema XXIII from *Atalanta Fugiens* by Michael Meyer (Frankfort, 1617).

Page 7, Figure 11: Detail from the Rupestrian Series by Raquel Mendieta Harrington, 1981.

Figure 12: Doni of Willendorf. Bronze copy by Nicky Oosterbaan, 1995. Height 10 cm. Photograph by Rufus C. Camphausen, 1995.

Figure 13: Cyrene Venus, second century B.C.E., Rome. National Museum of the Terme.

Figure 14: Object from Zaire, c. 1890. Height 14.5 cm. Vincent Dame Collection, Amsterdam. Photograph by Remus Dame, 1995.

Figure 15: Rock incisions from La Ferrassie (Leroi-Gourhan, *Préhistoire de l'art occidental*).

Figure 16: Doni of Laussel (24,000 B.C.E.), limestone relief found southeast of Perigueux, Dordogne, France.

Figure 40: Tripur Bhairavi. Painting by Harish Johari from *Tools for Tantra* (Rochester, Vt.: Destiny Books, 1986).

Figure 41: *Maria and Child*. Painting by Carlo Crivelli. National Gallery, London.

Figure 42: Argha. Height 30 cm. Vincent Dame Collection, Amsterdam. Photograph by Remus Dame, 1995.

Figure 43: Birds-eye view of Glastonbury (Osman, *Heilige Plaatsen*).

Figure 44: Votive tablet. Museum of Fine Arts, Boston (INV. 08.34b).

Figure 45: Silver pendant, Ethiopia. Height 1.8 cm. Vincent Dame Collection, Amsterdam. Photograph by Remus Dame, 1995.

Figure 46: Ivory pendant, Zaire. 8.7 cm. x 5.8 cm. Vincent Dame Collection, Amsterdam. Photograph by Remus Dame, 1995.

Figure 47: Bone amulet, Zaire. Height 7.6 cm. Vincent Dame Collection, Amsterdam. Photograph by Remus Dame, 1995.

Figure 48: Wooden stamp, India. Height 8.7 cm. Vincent Dame Collection, Amsterdam. Photograph by Remus Dame, 1995.

Page 36, Figure 49: Marble sculpture (c. 6,000 B.C.E.) from former Yugoslavia. Height 7.5 cm. (Gimbutas, *Goddesses and Gods of Old Europe*).

Figure 50: Eighth-century stone sculpture in the Museum of Alampur, India. 100 cm. x 90 cm. Archeological Survey of India.

Figure 51: *Flower of Passion*. Drawing by Christina Camphausen, 1995. Color pencil on paper, 22 cm. x 12 cm.

Figure 52: Kamakhya Pitha, Gauhati, Assam. Photograph by Annelies Rigter, 1995.

Figure 53: Mahasukhasiddhi. Computer-aided drawing (after a Tibetan original) by Rufus C. Camphausen, 1995.

Figure 54: Vajra Yogini. Drawing by Robert Beer, 1984.

Figure 55: Japanese terra-cotta (Camphausen, *Encyclopedia of Erotic Wisdom*).

Figure 56: Southeastern corner of the Kaaba. Drawing by Christina Camphausen, 1995. Pencil on paper, 18.8 cm. x 17.3 cm.

Page 51, Figure 57: Wooden statue, Burkina Faso, Upper Volta, Africa. Height 42 cm. Vincent Dame Collection, Amsterdam. Photograph by Remus Dame, 1995.

Figure 58: Ancestor spirit from Pulau, Micronesia. Hamburgisches Museum für Völkerkunde, Hamburg.

Figure 59: Sheela from Kilsarkan. Photograph by Anthony Weir, n.d.

Figure 60: Tokudashi scene (Camphausen, *Encyclopedia of Erotic Wisdom*).

Figure 61: Illustration by Charles Eisen for a story by La Fontaine.

Figure 62: Carved wood on door, Timor, Indonesia. Height 50 cm. Vincent Dame Collection, Amsterdam. Photograph by Remus Dame, 1995.

Figure 63: Rock painting from Tassili in the Sahara, Africa (Camphausen, *Encyclopedia of Erotic Wisdom*).

Figure 64: Terra-cotta figure of Baubo. Museum für Völkerkunde, Berlin.

Figure 91: *Surrounded Islands.* Christo and Jeanne-Claude, 1983.

Figure 92: *The Figure Hon.* Sculpture by Niki de Saint Phalle, 1966. 23.5 meters long, 10 meters wide, 6 meters high.

Figure 93: *Lulu.* Painting by Gottfried Helnwein, 1988. Watercolor on cardboard, 63 cm. x 55 cm.

Figure 94: *Erotic Earth (Terre Erotique).* Drawing by Andre Masson, 1939. Ink on paper, 31.5 cm. x 49 cm.

Figure 95: *Cosmic Egg* by Vincent Dame. Glazed ceramics, height 50 cm. Galerie Vignet, Amsterdam. Photograph by Remus Dame, 1995.

Figure 96: Yoni. Photograph by Christina Camphausen, 1994.

Figure 97: The Female Genital System. Drawing by Christina Camphausen, 1995. Pencil on paper, 14.3 cm. x 14 cm.

INDEX